PHYSICS
by Example

PHYSICS
by Example

Tim Prichard

First published 2019

Copyright © Tim Prichard 2019

The right of Tim Prichard to be identified as the author of this work has been asserted in accordance with the Copyright, Designs & Patents Act 1988.

All rights reserved. No part of this book may be reproduced, stored in a retrieval system, or transmitted in any form or by any means, electronic, electrostatic, magnetic tape, mechanical, photocopying, recording or otherwise, without the written permission of the copyright holder.

Published under licence by Brown Dog Books and
The Self-Publishing Partnership, 7 Green Park Station, Bath BA1 1JB

www.selfpublishingpartnership.co.uk

ISBN printed book: 978-1-83952-034-1
ISBN e-book: 978-1-83952-035-8

Cover design by Andrew Prescott
Internal design by Jenny Watson Design
Illustrations by Jasmine Cottage Marketing

Printed and bound by CPI Group (UK) Ltd, Croydon, CR0 4YY

This book is printed on FSC certified paper

CONTENTS

ENERGY 1
Energy transformations 1
The conservation of energy 2
Energy and work done 3
Gravitational Potential Energy (GPE) 5
Kinetic Energy (KE) 8
Elastic Potential Energy and Hooke's Law 11
Efficiency 14
Movement of heat and energy resources 20
Alternative energy resources 22
Specific heat capacity 24

ELECTRICITY 29
Static electricity 29
Electric current 30
Current, voltage and electrical resistance 31
Ohm's Law 32
Series and parallel circuits 34
Domestic electricity 38
Electrical power 39
Magnets and electricity 43
Magnetism produced by an electric current 44
The electric motor 47
Generators and making electricity from movement and magnetism 50
Alternators 51
Transformers 52
Current and power in transformers 54

RADIOACTIVITY AND MATTER — 59

Radioactivity and matter	59
Matter	74
Density	74
The Gas Laws	77
Charles' Law	79
The combined gas equation	82
Change of state	84
Latent heat	85
Specific latent heat of fusion	86

FORCES — 92

Scalar and vector quantities	92
What happens if forces act at an angle to each other?	94
Resolving forces in two components (vertical and horizontal)	97
Newton's laws of motion	99
Moments and turning forces	100
Gears	105
Centre of mass (gravity)	107
Motion graphs	111
Acceleration	115
Newton's second law and its relationship between force, mass and acceleration	120
Momentum	129
Momentum and collisions	131
The force of impact during a collision	133
Pressure	139
Pressure in liquids	142

WAVES — 148

Reflection	154
Colours of light and lenses	159

SPACE AND THE UNIVERSE — 166

Red shift	168
Background microwave radiation	169

ENERGY

Energy transformations

The conservation of energy:

"Energy can't be created or destroyed but only changed from one form into another."

Explain the energy changes for the following situations:

1) A stone falling off a ledge.
2) A light bulb being switched on.
3) An electric car moving.
4) Switching on a battery-operated fan.

Answers:

1) GPE → KE → sound + thermal

    GPE = gravitational potential energy (energy because of an object's height/position)

    KE = kinetic energy (movement energy)

    > Note: the stone is high up so it has GPE, it falls so it is moving (KE), then hits the floor/ground which you can hear and heat will be lost to the surroundings.

2) Electrical → light + heat

    > Note: light bulbs get hot as a lot of energy is lost as heat.

3) Chemical → electrical → KE

    > Note: batteries (cells) are a store of chemical energy which is converted into electricity in the wires of the device.

4) Chemical → electrical → KE

    > Key point: heat is always lost in an energy transformation.

The conservation of energy

1) What energy changes happen when a pendulum swings?
2) Describe the energy changes when a bungee jumper jumps off a bridge.

Answers:

1) At the top of the swing or start, the pendulum 'bob' has 100% gravitational potential energy (GPE). As the 'bob' swings down it gains kinetic energy (KE) because it is increasing in speed. When the 'bob' is at the bottom of the swing, for a moment in time it has 100% KE and no potential energy (PE). As it starts to swing upwards, the KE decreases and PE starts to increase. Halfway up or down the swing the pendulum has 50% KE and 50% PE.

> Note: You may be asked why the pendulum stops swinging. This is due to air resistance pushing against the pendulum and also friction at the top of the pendulum. You can call air resistance 'drag', but air resistance is more accurate.

2) In the very first moment the jumper has 100% GPE. As soon as the jumper starts accelerating towards the Earth GPE starts to decrease and KE increases. The rope becomes tight, slowing the jumper down, so KE decreases but as the rope stretches, its own elastic energy increases. This elastic energy continues to increase until the jumper reaches the bottom of the jump or maximum length of the bungee cord. For an instant the KE is *zero*, GPE is *zero* and all the energy has been transferred to elastic potential energy. The jumper then starts to move back upwards so KE increases, as does GPE. GPE will not reach its initial value as the jumper would not reach the start height. This is because energy will be dissipated to the surroundings due to air resistance and a small amount of heat loss through friction.

Energy and work done

energy is the ability to do work.

When energy is transferred, work is done.

The formula for work done is:

    Work done = force × distance moved

This can be put into a triangular relationship as follows:

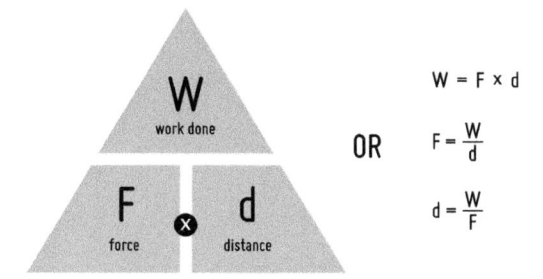

$$W = F \times d$$

OR

$$F = \frac{W}{d}$$

$$d = \frac{W}{F}$$

Examples

1) A builder lifts a 25 kg bag of cement onto a lorry 1.5 m high. How much work did he do lifting the cement?

   Answer:
   Work = force × distance moved

       = (25 × 10) × 1.5

       = 250 × 1.5

       = **375 Joules**

   Note: We have to change the mass in kg into a force in newtons by multiplying the mass by 10, which is the effect of gravity. The question will tell you gravity is 10 or more accurately 9.8 m/s^2.

2) How much work would be done pushing a shopping trolley with 15 kg of shopping in it 300 m around a shop?

   Answer:
   Work = force × distance moved

       = (15 × 10) × 300

       = 45,000 Joules or **45 kJ**

   Note: We can use the prefix 'k' for kilo meaning 1000, so we do not need to use the three zeros in the first answer.

4 ENERGY | *Energy and work done*

3) If a water-skier was pulled with a force of 700 N across a lake and the work done was 420 kJ, how far was the water-skier pulled?

Answer:
Rearrange: $W = F \times D$ to $D = \dfrac{W}{F}$

So: $D = \dfrac{W}{F} = 420 \text{ kJ}/700 \text{ N} = 600 \text{ m}$

> Note: again we had to change the 420 kJ into 420,000 J to get the answer in metres.

4) A student calculated she used 26.1 Joules of energy when she lifted a 3 kg mass onto a table. How high was the table?

Answer:
Distance $= \dfrac{W}{F} = \dfrac{26.1}{30} = 0.87$ m or **87 cm**

5) What force is required to move a pile of books 50 cm if the work done is 300 J?

Answer:
Force $= \dfrac{W}{D} = \dfrac{300}{0.5} = $ **600 N**

> Note: the distance in cm is changed to metres, e.g. 0.5 m.

6) A shop worker lifts a box of 12 bags of sugar onto a shelf. If each bag has a mass of 1 kg and the work done is 240 Joules, how high is the shelf?

Answer:
First total mass $= 12 \times 1$ kg
$= 12$ kg
$= 12 \times 10$
$= 120$ Newtons

Distance $= \dfrac{W}{F} = \dfrac{240 \text{ J}}{120 \text{ N}} = $ **2 m**

> Note: first calculate the total mass, then force in N by multiplying by gravity (10).

Gravitational Potential Energy (GPE)

This is energy an object has because of its height or position. This means the higher up or more unbalanced an object is, the greater its GPE.

To calculate GPE we use the formula:

Gravitational potential energy = mass × gravity × change in height

GPE = m × g × h

> **Note: GPE is a form of energy so it is measured in Joules. I am using gravity which is short for gravitational field strength. This is a force of 10 N/kg acting downwards.**

1) A ball of mass 0.5 kg is kicked 20 m into the air. At the top of its journey, how much GPE does it have?

   > Note: g = 10

   Answer:
   GPE = m × g × h
   = 0.5 × 10 × 20
   = 100 J

2) How much GPE does 2 kg of water have if it flows over a 75 m waterfall? Assume the waterfall is vertical and gravity is 10 N/kg.

   Answer:
   GPE = m × g × h
   = 2 × 10 × 75
   = 1500 J

3) A ball is dropped from 2 m onto the ground. It bounces back to a height of 1.9 m. Calculate the GPE both at the start and when it bounced back to 1.9 m. The ball has a mass of 160 g, and gravity is 10 N/kg.

   > Note: the mass has to be changed into kg by dividing by 1000 g. The mass is therefore 0.16 kg.

6 ENERGY | *Gravitational Potential Energy (GPE)*

Answer:
At the start –

GPE = m × g × h
    = 0.16 × 10 × 2
    = **3.2 Joules**

At the bounce height –

GPE = m × g × h
    = 0.16 × 10 × 1.9
    = **3.04 Joules**

> Note: The difference in energy is 0.16 Joules. This means energy has been lost to the surroundings.

4) a) Three people are in a lift. If the lift moves up to the sixth floor, how much GPE do the people have in total?

   b) When the lift returns to the ground floor, how much GPE does it have?

   Data for calculations:

   Person 1 = 76 kg, Person 2 = 80 kg, Person 3 = 98 kg

   Gravity = 10 N/kg

   Ignore the mass of the lift

   Each floor has a height of 3 m

   Answers:
   a) GPE = mgh

   Total mass = 76 kg + 80 kg + 98 kg
             = **254 kg**

   Total height gained at sixth floor = 6 × 3 = 18 m

   Total GPE on sixth floor = 254 × 10 × 18
                            = **45,720 J or 45.72 kJ**

   b) The answer would be zero. This is because h is zero as the lift is on the ground, and m and g are multiplied by zero.

5) If an aeroplane and its passengers have a total mass of 250,000 kg, and taking gravitational field strength to be 10 N/kg, calculate the height it is travelling at to have a GPE of 5×10^9 J.

Answer:
GPE = mgh

5×10^9 J = 250,000 × 10 × h

5,000,000,000 = 2,500,000 × h

$h = \dfrac{5 \times 10^9}{2.5 \times 10^6}$

= **2000 m or 2 km**

Note: I have used "standard form" to represent the energy and mass because the numbers are so large.

Kinetic Energy (KE)

Kinetic energy is the energy an object has because of its movement. The amount of energy depends upon the mass of the object and its velocity. It is measured in Joules (J), mass in (kg) and velocity in metres per second (m/s).

The formula for calculating kinetic energy (KE) is:

Kinetic energy = ½ × mass × velocity squared
KE = ½ mv²

> **Note:** A common problem students have with this formula is the "squared" bit. Only velocity is squared, not the whole equation. To help students I often tell them to solve the calculation backwards, so they square velocity first, then multiply by the mass, then multiply by a ½ or divide the answer by two.

1) A car of mass 850 kg is moving at 15 m/s. Calculate its kinetic energy.

   Answer:
   KE = ½ mv²

       = ½ × 850 × (15)²

       = ½ × 850 × 225

       = **95,625 Joules** or **95.62 kJ**

2) A motorcycle of mass 250 kg is moving at 6 m/s. What is its KE?

   Answer:
   KE = ½ mv²

       = 1/2 × 250 × (6)²

       = ½ × 250 × 36

       = **4500 J**

3) A car of mass 1200 kg comes to a sudden stop when the brakes are applied. If the energy required by the brakes is 173,400 Joules, how fast was it moving just before the brakes were applied?

Answer:
$E = \frac{1}{2} mv^2$

$173,400 = \frac{1}{2} \times 1200 \times v^2$

$173,400 = 600 \times v^2$

$v^2 = \frac{173,400}{600} = 289$

$v = \sqrt{289}$

$v = \mathbf{17\ m/s}$

4) A lorry is moving at 30 m/s along a motorway. If it has 1,575,000 Joules of kinetic energy, what is its mass? (Assume no energy is lost to the surroundings for the purposes of this question.)

Answer:
$E = \frac{1}{2} mv^2$

$1,575,000 = \frac{1}{2} \times m \times (30)^2$

$1,575,000 = \frac{1}{2} \times m \times 900$

$1,575,000 = 450 \times m$

$m = \frac{1,575,000}{450}$

$m = \mathbf{3500\ kg}$

ENERGY | *Kinetic Energy (KE)*

5) If a small car of 1000 kg is travelling at 10 m/s and increases its speed to 20 m/s, how many times does the kinetic energy increase?

Answer:
Remember in the equation, $KE = \frac{1}{2}mv^2$, the velocity is squared. So if you ignore m (mass), as the mass of the car does not change, and ignore the ½, then:

Suppose v = 2 then v² = 2 × 2 = 4

If v is doubled as in the question to 4, v = 4 so v² = 4 × 4 = 16

Therefore:

$\frac{16}{4}$ = 4 so the kinetic energy increases by 4 (or × 4)

You could check this by doing the actual calculations as below:

At the start the velocity of the car is 10 m/s, so:

KE = ½ mv²

    = ½ × 1000 × (10)²

    = **50,000 Joules**

The car increases its speed to 20 m/s

KE = ½ mv²

    = ½ × 1000 × (20)²

    = **200,000 Joules**

Check your answer:

$\frac{200,000}{50,000}$ = 4

(i.e. the KE has increased × 4)

Elastic Potential Energy and Hooke's Law

Whenever something is stretched and it displays elastic behaviour (when held under tension) it is said to have elastic potential energy. Common examples are stretched springs or elastic bands. This means when they are not relaxed they will try to move back to their original position. This is true for materials which follow Hooke's law. Some materials may not return to their original position and do not follow Hooke's law.

In a nutshell: the more you pull a spring, the longer it gets.

Hooke's law states:

"The force is proportional to the spring constant multiplied by the extension."

i.e. the extension is proportional to the force applied. This would produce a graph like:

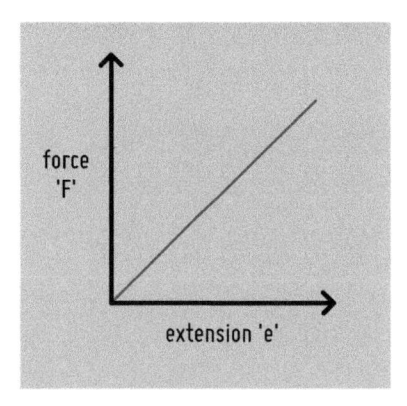

[Graph showing force 'F' on y-axis vs extension 'e' on x-axis as a straight line through origin]

Because it is directly proportional it produces a straight line graph. This means the material extends by the same amount each time a force is added of the same amount. Or: double the force = double the extension!

The equation is:

$F = ke$

Force = spring constant × extension

k, the spring constant, is specific to a material or depends upon its construction (stiffness). It can be thought of as the force per unit extension of the spring pulling the spring back to rest.

The elastic potential energy is the energy stored in a stretched spring/band etc.

To calculate elastic potential energy we use the equation:

$E_e = \frac{1}{2} ke^2$

$(J) = \frac{1}{2} (N/m)(m)$

ENERGY | *Elastic Potential Energy and Hooke's Law*

> Note: The equation for Ee is very similar to the formula for kinetic energy. To solve problems always square extension e only, not the whole equation. See note for KE.

1) Find the spring constant 'k' for a spring if 600 N is required to stretch it 15 cm.

   Answer:
   $$f = -ke$$
   $$k = \frac{f}{e}$$
   $$= \frac{600}{0.15}$$
   $$= 4000 \text{ N/m}$$

   > Note: The units of 'k' (spring constant) are Newtons per metre, as it is calculated from force ÷ extension.

2) A spring has a constant of k = 9500 N/m. If it is stretched by a force of 2500 N, calculate its extension from rest (equilibrium).

   Answer:
   $$f = -ke$$
   $$e = \frac{f}{k}$$
   $$= \frac{2500}{9500}$$
   $$= 0.263 \text{ m or } 26.3 \text{ cm}$$

   > Note: The formula has a minus because it shows the spring is stretched and is trying to move back to rest or its normal unstretched size/position.

3) Calculate the elastic potential energy for a spring when it is stretched 0.25 m and the spring constant is 2000 N/m.

   Answer:
   $$Ee = \frac{1}{2} ke^2$$
   $$= \frac{1}{2} \times 2000 \times (0.25)^2$$
   $$= \frac{1}{2} \times 2000 \times 0.0625$$
   $$= 62.5 \text{ Joules}$$

4) A car has a mass of 1600 kg. With this load the car has a maximum compression of 0.15 m when stationary. Calculate:

   a) The spring constant, assuming gravity 'g' = 10 N/m.

   b) How much elastic potential energy each spring would have when compressed if the mass were increased to 1900 kg because some passengers got into the car and the springs compressed another 0.1 m.

Answers:

a) Note Newton's second law, f = ma (force = mass × acceleration) and the 1600 kg is spread evenly over each wheel (four wheels). So each wheel has 400 kg acting on it.

Force on each wheel:

f = ma

$\quad$ = 400 × 10

$\quad$ = **4000 N**

using f = -ke (Hooke's law):

4000 = k × 0.15

$k = \dfrac{4000}{-0.15}$

$\quad$ = 26666.6 recurring

k = **27 kN/m**

b) First calculate the total compression of the car:

(compression due to car's own weight) + (compression due to passengers) = (total compression)

0.15 m + 0.1 m = 0.25 m

Ee = ½ ke²

$\quad$ = ½ × 26666.6 × (0.25)²

$\quad$ = ½ × 26666.6 × 0.0625

$\quad$ = **833.3 Joules**

Efficiency

When thinking about efficiency, the first thing to consider is what useful operation/energy is gained from a device or process, and what is wasted. For example, think to yourself, 'What is a light bulb for?' or 'What is a radio for?'

Examples of useful and wasted energy:

Object	Useful energy	Wasted energy
Light bulb	Light	Heat
Washing machine	KE + heat	Heat + sound
Electric drill	KE	Heat + sound

Next we need to realise that efficiency is measured as a percentage and has no units.

The formula to calculate efficiency is as follows:

$$\text{Efficiency} = \frac{\text{Useful output from a device}}{\text{Useful input supplied to device}} \times 100\%$$

$$\text{Put simply} = \frac{\text{what you get out}}{\text{what you put in}} \times 100\%$$

Things to consider when answering questions about efficiency:

Firstly, when thinking about wasted energy, heat is nearly always lost to the surroundings. So if you are answering a question about what type of energy is lost to the surroundings, heat is always a good answer to use.

Secondly, when calculating efficiency, the answer should always be less than one before you multiply by 100 or your answer will be greater than 100%!

My advice to students is: "always divide the smaller number by the larger number if you are not sure what to do".

1) A small electric toy's motor is supplied with 150 J of energy. If the toy uses 90 J of energy to move across the floor, what is the efficiency of the motor?

   Answer:

   $$\text{efficiency} = \frac{\text{output}}{\text{input}} \times 100$$

   $$\frac{90}{150} \times 100 = 60$$

   efficiency = **60%**

2) A tennis ball is dropped out of a window 7 m high. The ball has a mass of 58 g. The ball bounces back to a height of 2.87 m. Calculate the ball's bounce efficiency. Assume gravity = 10 N/kg.

Answer:

Consider the change in GPE (Gravitational Potential Energy).

GPE at drop height = mass × gravity × height

= 0.058 kg × 10 N/kg × 7 m

= 4.06 Joules

GPE at bounce height = m × g × h

= 0.058 × 10 × 2.87

GPE = 1.66 J

bounce efficiency = $\frac{GPE\ bounce\ height}{GPE\ drop\ height}$ × 100%

= $\frac{1.66}{4.06}$ × 100%

Bounce efficiency = **40.88%**

> Note: Because the mass of the tennis ball and gravity don't change, they can be ignored in the calculation, but the answer will be slightly less accurate.

e.g. $\frac{bounce\ height}{drop\ height}$ × 100%

= $\frac{2.87}{7.00}$ × 100%

= **41%**

3) A builder pulls a 20 kg block up a 15 m slope with a force of 180 N, gaining a total height of 12 m. Calculate the energy wasted and the efficiency of this process.

Energy used = force × distance moved

= 180 N × 15 m

Energy used = 2700 J

GPE gained = mass × gravity × height

= 20 kg × 10 N/kg × 12 m

GPE gained = 2400 J

Energy wasted = 2700 J − 2400 J

= **300 Joules**

Efficiency = $\frac{2400}{2700}$ × 100%

= **88.8%**

16 ENERGY | *Efficiency*

4) An electric light bulb produces 300 J/s of light, but it was supplied with 1200 J/s of electrical energy.

   a) Calculate the efficiency of the light bulb.
   b) Suggest why the light bulb is not 100% efficient.

   Answer:

   a) Efficiency = $\dfrac{\text{useful energy output}}{\text{total energy input}} \times 100\%$

   $= \dfrac{300}{1200} \times 100\%$

   $= 25\%$

   b) Electric light bulbs become very hot, so 75% of the electrical energy supplied in this example is lost as heat. This is why people are now using much more efficient low-wattage LED lights.

   > Note: The J/s or joule-second is also known as the watt, which is the unit of power. It is a measure of how much energy is used per second.

5) An electric motor produces 8000 J of work. How much energy must be supplied if its efficiency were:

   a) 75%
   b) 60%

   Answers:

   a) Efficiency = $\dfrac{\text{useful output}}{\text{total input}} \times 100\%$

   $0.75 = \dfrac{8000}{\text{energy supplied}} \times 100\%$

   energy supplied = $\dfrac{8000}{0.75}$

   $= 10666.6 \text{ Joules}$

   b) Efficiency = $\dfrac{\text{useful output}}{\text{total input}} \times 100\%$

   $0.6 = \dfrac{8000}{\text{energy supplied}} \times 100\%$

   Energy supplied = $\dfrac{8000}{0.6}$

   $= 13333.3 \text{ Joules}$

   > Note: the 75% and 60% are converted into the decimal forms

Short revision of energy and efficiency

1) State the law of conservation of energy

2) Describe the energy transformations in the following situations or devices, and also name the energy wasted:
   a) loudspeaker playing music
   b) lifting a dumbbell in a gym
   c) a kettle boiling water

3) Which type of energy is usually lost to the surroundings during energy transformations?

4) Calculate the work done in moving a 25 kg object 15 m.

5) A force of 17 N was needed to pull a shopping trolley along the aisle of a supermarket and the work done was 340 Joules. How long was the aisle?

6) How much GPE does a 2 kg object have if it is held 3 m off the ground? (take gravity to be 10 N/kg)

7) Calculate the force of a 500 g ball moving at 7 m/s.

8) What is the velocity of a mountain bike if it is moving with a kinetic energy of 337.5 Joules and has a mass of 12 kg? (ignore the mass of the rider)

9) A spring is stretched 3 cm. If the spring constant is 2500 N/m calculate the size of the force needed to produce this extension.

10) Find the elastic potential energy (E_e) when a spring is stretched 37 cm if the spring has a constant of 1250 N/m.

11) What is the efficiency of a hair dryer if it is supplied with 2000 J/s of electrical energy, but only 500 J of energy is converted into useful energy? (KE + heat)

12) A ball is dropped off the top of Blackpool Tower which is 158 m high. If the ball bounces back to a height of 27.5 m, how efficient was the bounce of the ball?

1) Energy can't be created or destroyed, only transferred. ✓

2) a) Electrical → Sound ✓
   b) Chemical → kinetic ✗
   c) Electrical → heat ✓

3) Heat ✓

4) $W = Fs$
   $25 \times 15 = 375 J$ ✗

5) $340/17 = 20m$ ✓

6) $2 \times 3 \times 10 = 60 J$ ✓

7) $\frac{1}{2} \times 0.5 \times 7^2 = 12.25 J$ ✓

8) $337.5 = \frac{1}{2} \times 12 \times \_^2$
   $\sqrt{337.5 / \frac{1}{2} / 12} = 7.5 m/s$ ✓

9) $0.03 \times 2500 = 75 N$ ✓

10) $\frac{1}{2} \times 1250 \times 0.37^2 = 85.6 J$ ✓

11) $500/2000 \times 100 = 25\%$ ✓

12) $27.5 / 158 \times 100 = 17.4\%$ ✓

Answers:

1) Energy cannot be created or destroyed, only converted from one form to another.

2) (a) Electrical → sound

   (b) Chemical → kinetic energy → gravitational potential energy

   (c) Electrical → heat

3) Heat.

4) $w = f \times D$

   $= 250 \times 15$

   3750 J

5) $w = f \times D$

   $D = \dfrac{w}{f} = \dfrac{340}{17}$

   $= 20\text{ m}$

6) $GPE = mgh$

   $= 2 \times 10 \times 3$

   $= 60\text{ J}$

7) $½\,mv^2 = ½ \times 0.5 \times 7^2$

   $= 12.25\text{ J}$

8) 7.5 m/s

9) $f = KE = 0.03 \times 2500$

   $= 75\text{ N}$

10) $E_e = ½\,ke^2$

    $= ½ \times 1250 \times (0.37)^2$

    $= 85.6\text{ J}$

11) 25%

12) 17.4%

Movement of heat and energy resources

Briefly, the main points to consider about heat transfer are:

a) Heat travels by three methods: conduction, convection, and radiation.

b) Conduction moves through materials, convection by moving gases or liquids, and radiation as an electromagnetic wave.

c) Heat can only move from a hot place to a cool place.

d) Heat moves at different rates through materials and this is called thermal conductivity.

e) Insulators stop the movement of heat. They can keep things warm or cold.

> **Note point (e) – students often forget things can be kept cold using insulation, not just hot!**

1) Water is heated using the solar panel below:

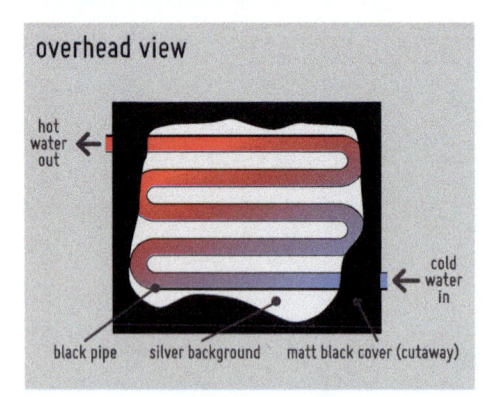

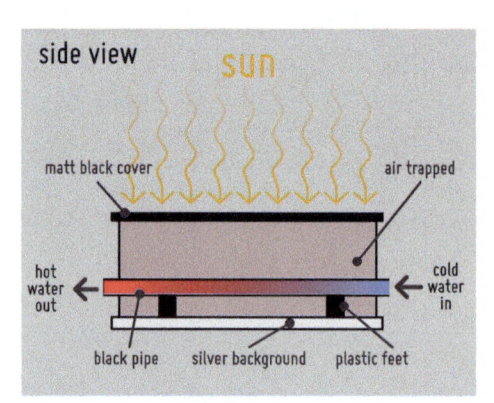

a) Explain how each feature helps the solar panel to heat water.
b) How would using an evacuated panel help improve heat loss?

Answer

1) a) Explain how each feature helps the solar panel to heat water.

   Matt black cover
   Black is a very good absorber of heat, and being matt this also helps to improve the amount of heat absorbed. The cover also traps heat in the panel, and reduces heat loss by convection.

   Air trapped
   Air is a good insulator of heat as it is a poor conductor, so it helps to trap heat in the panel.

   Black water pipes
   Again, being black means the pipes will absorb heat and transfer this by conduction to the water.

   Plastic feet
   Plastic is a poor conductor of heat so they stop heat loss from the pipes, as they don't touch the panel casing.

   Silver lining
   Silver is a good reflector of heat, so any heat in the panel will be reflected back into the panel and onto the pipes. It will help to heat up the water.

   b) Using a vacuum in the panel will reduce heat loss by convection and conduction more, as there are no particles to conduct or move by convection.

2) Why do people in hot countries like Greece and Spain traditionally paint their houses white?

> Note: Most students when asked this question only think about in the day when the temperature is warmer, but we also need to consider the cooler evening and night-time.

Answer:
White is a good reflector and poor absorber of heat so it will reflect the heat of the Sun in the day, keeping the building cooler inside. If the walls are made of thick stone, they will, however, heat up slowly. This is beneficial because at night the walls will act as a heat storage, keeping the inside warmer. Also the white outside is a poor radiator of heat meaning the house will lose heat slowly over the evening and night. This is because white, bright colours are poor radiators of heat.

Alternative energy resources

Alternative energy resources refer to energy resources which are not based on the fossil fuels coal, oil and natural gas. We often refer to them as 'renewables' or renewable resources. Nuclear power is included in this section but it is not renewable as it uses nuclear fuel; it is not a fossil fuel, however.

Questions on this topic are generally similar in the fact they ask you about the good and bad points of renewable and nuclear technology, where you would use each source and compare them to fossil fuels.

> Note: A big mistake students make is they will often state that renewable energy is 'free'. IT IS NOT! The source of energy is free, e.g. waves, wind and sunlight, but the cost of developing, maintaining, and materials can be very expensive, especially when the technology is new.

1) a) Explain what is meant by renewable energy.
   b) Describe the advantages and disadvantages of renewable energy.

Answer:
1) a) Renewable energy is a resource which will never run out as they are naturally replaced, e.g. wind or waves. Non-renewable resources like coal are not replaceable because once they are used they are gone forever.

> Note: The processes involved in making coal, oil and gas take millions of years so they are considered non-renewable.

   b) This question is best summarised in a table like the one below:

Advantages	Disadvantages
• Never run out • Don't produce 'greenhouse gases' • Don't contribute to 'acid rain' • No dangerous waste material • Can be used 'off-grid' in remote areas • Don't need to be part of national network	• Low power output • Unreliable, e.g. solar does not work at night! • Unsightly • No single source meets full demand • Can use up large areas of land • Can damage habitats, e.g. estuaries

2) Compare nuclear power and solar power

   Answer:
   Nuclear power is a constant source of energy, whereas solar is variable depending upon the amount of UV light available. Weather conditions effect solar greatly and they don't work at night. Nuclear power is not affected by weather.

   Nuclear power does not produce greenhouse gases or contribute to acid rain; solar power also does not. However, nuclear power does produce dangerous or harmful waste products which have to be managed carefully. Solar power produces no waste.

Nuclear power stations are very expensive to build and maintain so the capital costs are very high.

Solar panels are much cheaper to manufacture and maintain.

Nuclear power needs a lot of infrastructure and needs to be part of a grid system, whereas solar can be totally individual, small-scale and placed anywhere, even in remote areas like the Australian outback.

Solar panels produce small amounts of power so a lot of panels are needed to produce useable energy on a large scale. This means solar farms tend to cover large areas. Nuclear power produces very large amounts of energy even though they also cover a large area.

Nuclear power can take up to three days to start up or shut down. It needs to run constantly. Solar power is instant provided there is enough light.

3) a) Explain what is meant by a biofuel and why they are considered renewable.
   b) What is meant by the term 'carbon-neutral'.

   Answer:
   a) Biofuels are fuels which have come from living organisms, waste products from living organisms, or dead and decaying material. Examples are ethanol from fermented sugar cane and methane gas from decaying rubbish and pig, cow or chicken manure. There are many other examples. They are considered renewable because they are either regrown, as in the case of sugar cane, or continuously replaced like manure or rubbish being produced by man.

   b) Carbon-neutral: This is a recent concept which in theory suggests that a plant, for example, removes carbon from the atmosphere as carbon dioxide, which is then replaced back into the atmosphere when that plant is burnt or decays, producing carbon dioxide and methane gas. The overall, or net, amount of carbon dioxide in the atmosphere is therefore zero, or the same.

4) Why can Iceland and New Zealand use geothermal energy as a major source of energy, whereas France and the UK can't?

   Answer:
   Geothermal energy is highly specific to areas of volcanic activity. If a country is not in an area of volcanic or geological activity, then it is not feasible to use this sort of renewable energy. New Zealand and Iceland are near or on areas of tectonic activity which are volcanic and are undergoing a lot of geological change. Geothermal energy comes from heat which is released by radioactive substances deep within the Earth's crust. Water is pumped down into the crust, turns into steam and is then recaptured to drive turbines to produce electricity.

Specific heat capacity

Heat capacity of a substance is a relatively simple concept. It is a measure of how much energy is needed to raise the temperature of a material. Specific heat capacity simply considers how much energy is needed to raise 1 kg of a substance by 1°C. This allows us to compare materials and calculate exactly how much energy is needed for a particular energy change.

Formula:

Energy transferred	=	mass	×	specific heat capacity	×	temperature change
ΔE		= m	×	c	×	$\Delta \theta$
Joules		kg		J/kg°C		°C

Note: Δ = delta, a Greek letter, used to represent 'change in'

This can be rearranged to:

$$c = \frac{\Delta E}{m \Delta \theta}$$

Note: The more particles there are in a solid, liquid or gas, the more energy is required to raise its temperature.

1) Calculate the specific heat capacity for water in an experiment using these figures:
   - kettle has a power rating of 2500 watts (2500 joules a second)
   - mass of water is 1.2 kg
   - time kettle switched on = 2 min = 120 seconds
   - temperature rise = 60°C

   Answer:
   The energy supplied = power in watts × time (seconds)

   = 2500 × 120

   = 300,000 Joules

   Energy for 1 kg = energy ÷ mass

   = $\frac{300,000}{1.2}$

   = **250,000 Joules**

Specific heat capacity is the energy per degrees Celsius so,

250,000 ÷ 60°C

= **4167 J/kg°C**

> Note: the actual figure for water is 4200 J/kg°C. Heat energy is always lost to the surroundings so the experimental figure is always a little low. In an experiment the better the insulation, the better your calculation will be.

2) How much heat energy is needed to raise the temperature of 2 kg of aluminium from 10°C to 25°C? The specific heat capacity of Al = 900 J/kg°C

Answer:

$E = mc(\theta_2 - \theta_1)$

$E = 2 \times 900 \times (25-10)$

$E = 1800 \times 15$

$E = 27,000$ J

3) A 1.2 kg piece of copper is supplied with 6782.4 joules of heat energy from an electric heater. The temperature of the copper is raised by 15°C. Calculate the specific heat capacity of copper.

Answer:

$c = \dfrac{\Delta E}{m \Delta \theta}$

$c = \dfrac{6782.4}{1.2 \times 15}$

$c = 376.8$ J/kg°C

Short revision questions on renewable energy and specific heat capacity

1) What is meant by the term 'alternative energy resource', and give three examples?

2) Why are fossil fuels not considered renewable?

3) What are the main issues with fossil fuels?

4) Why should government policy include a range of renewable options?

5) State the equation which links specific heat capacity, energy, temperature and mass.

6) How much heat energy is needed to increase the temperature of a 4 kg block of aluminium from 20°C to 27°C? (SHC for Al = 900 J/kg)

1) Energy resources that aren't fossil fuels, including biofuel, tidal and wave energy

2) There is a limited amount; they will eventually run out

3) They are limited and produce greenhouse gases ✓ and acid rain

4) As options such as solar only works during the day, and options such as wind are intermittent and unreliable. ✓

5) $E = mc \times (\theta_2 - \theta_1)$

6) $4 \times 900 \times 7 = 25200$ J ✓

Answers:

1) An energy resource which is not coal, oil or natural gas. E.g. tidal, solar, wind, biofuel, hydroelectric, biofuels, wave.

2) Because they take millions of years to form.

3) Greenhouse gases, acid rain, limited resources running out.

4) They are not 100% reliable all of the time so a selection should be used so some electricity is always being produced.

5) $E = m \times c \times (\theta_2 - \theta_1)$

6) 25,200 J.

ELECTRICITY

Static electricity

Points to consider:

- static electricity is produced by friction.
- there are two types of charge: positive and negative
- only negative charges can move
- like charges repel, and unlike charges attract

1) Explain why rubbing a cloth on a strip of polythene produces a negative charge on the polythene.

   Answer:
   When the cloth rubs on the polythene strip, friction occurs between the two materials. Electrons (negatively charged particles) leave the cloth and are transferred onto the polythene strip. Because there are more negative charges than positive charges, the strip becomes negative overall.

2) Why do most materials have no static charge?

   Answer:
   When a material has no overall static charge, it is said to have equal numbers of positive and negative charges so it is called neutral. A material becomes charged when there is more of one charge than the other. Remember only negative charges can move, so the charge actually depends upon the number of electrons present compared to the stationary positive charges.

3) Explain why a balloon will stick to a wall when rubbed.

   Answer:
   First rubbing a balloon with a cloth will give it a static charge because of friction. For the purpose of this question assume the balloon becomes negative because it has gained electrons from the cloth. When it is brought near the wall the negative charges on the surface of the wall are repelled into the wall. This leaves the surface of the wall positive. The negative balloon and positive wall surface attract each other and the balloon sticks. If the balloon had gained a positive charge because it had lost electrons to the cloth, when it is brought close to the wall it would attract more electrons to the surface of the wall so the balloon would stick.

Electric current

A flow of charge is called a current. The current is measured in Amperes or Amps (A). The flow of charge is measured in a unit called the coulomb (C).

Note: A current of 1 ampere is the flow of 1 coulomb per second.

OR

$Q = I \times t$

Coulombs = Current × time

This can be placed in a formula triangle:

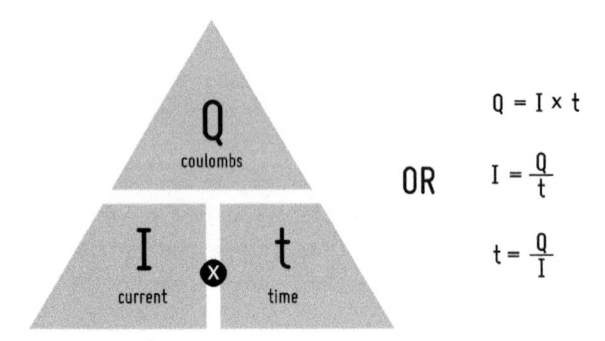

$Q = I \times t$

OR

$I = \frac{Q}{t}$

$t = \frac{Q}{I}$

1) In a simple circuit a current of 0.5 amps flows for 2 minutes. Calculate the flow of charge Q.

   Answer:
   First convert the minutes into seconds, so 2 min = 120 seconds. Then use the formula:

   $Q = I \times t$

   $Q = 0.5 \times 120$

   Q = 60 coulombs

2) Calculate the current through a lamp if 8 coulombs of charge flow for 90 seconds.

   Answer:
   $I = \frac{Q}{t}$

   $= \frac{80}{90}$

   = 0.88 amps

3) A torch used 120 coulombs of charge with a current of 0.2 amps. How long was the torch on for?

Answer:

$$t = \frac{Q}{I}$$

$$= \frac{120}{0.2}$$

$$= 600 \text{ seconds } (10 \text{ minutes})$$

Current, voltage and electrical resistance

Note: In physics, voltage and potential difference (or PD) both mean the same thing.

Ohm's Law

Ohm's law states that 'The current through a component is directly proportional to the voltage provided the temperature remains constant'.

This can be mathematically represented by:

V α I

V = voltage, I = current, α = 'proportional to', R = resistance

There is also a triangular relationship between V, I and R:

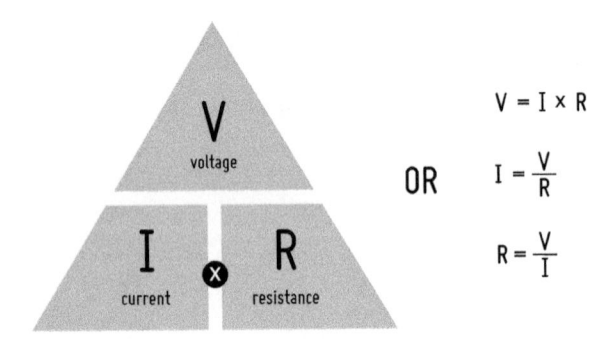

$$V = I \times R$$

OR

$$I = \frac{V}{R}$$

$$R = \frac{V}{I}$$

1) In a simple circuit a current is 0.7 amps flows and the voltage across the circuit is 5 volts.

   Calculate the resistance in that circuit.

   Answer:
   Use the relationship $R = \frac{V}{I}$

   $= \frac{5}{0.7}$

   $= 7.14 \, \Omega$ (ohms)

2) A kettle element has an electrical resistance of 25 Ω. If the mains voltage is 230 volts, calculate the current flowing in the kettle's element.

   Answer:
   Use the relationship $I = \frac{V}{R}$

   $= \frac{230}{25}$

   $= 9.2$ amps

3) A torch has a current of 1.8 amps flowing through it and a resistance of 3.33 ohms.

   Calculate the voltage of the cell in this torch.

Answer:
Use the relationship: V = I × R

= 1.8 × 3.33

= 5.99 or **6 volts**

4) Draw a current voltage graph for the following:

   a) lamp or bulb

   b) a long wire

   c) a diode

Answers:

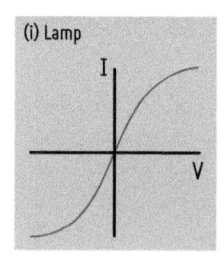

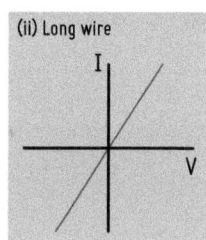

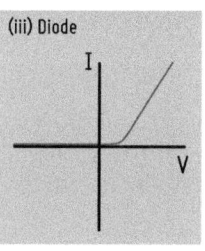

(i) Lamp   (ii) Long wire   (iii) Diode

Note:

a) The lamp's graph curves as it becomes hot and electrical resistance increases.

b) The long wire remains at a constant temperature so the current and voltage are always directly proportional. This means if you double the voltage the current doubles, or halving the voltage halves the current, etc.

c) The diode current remains at zero up to a point and then suddenly shoots up. This happens in the forward direction only.

5) In a diode the forward resistance is low but the resistance in the reverse direction is high. Is this true or false?

Answer:
True

6) A thermistor's resistance decreases as temperature increases. Is this true or false?

Answer:
True

7) The resistance of a light-dependent resistor (LDR) decreases as light intensity increases. Is this true or false?

Answer:
True

Series and parallel circuits

1) In the series circuit below a 6 V cell is connected to two resistors in series. The first resistor has a resistance of 3 ohms, and the second a resistance of 2 ohms. Calculate the current in the circuit.

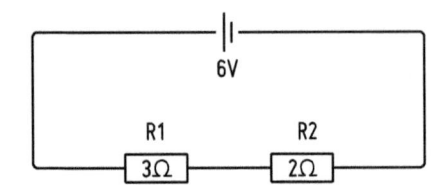

Answer:
First calculate the total resistance in the circuit, RT.

$R_T = R_1 + R_2$

$= 3 + 2$

$= 5$ ohms

Then use the relationship: $I = \dfrac{V}{R}$

$= \dfrac{6}{5}$

$= 1.2$ amps

2) Three 1.5 V cells are joined in series along with two bulbs in series. The first bulb has a resistance of 3 Ω, and the second has a resistance of 2.5 Ω. Calculate the current in the circuit.

Answer:
Total resistance $R_T = 3 + 2.5 = 5.5\ \Omega$

Total voltage $= 3 \times 1.5$

$= 4.5$ V

Using the relationship: $I = \dfrac{V}{R}$

$I = \dfrac{4.5}{5.5}$

$= 0.82$ amps

3) Look at the parallel circuit below and calculate the current through the 6 Ω resistor and the 10 Ω resistor. Then calculate the current through the 3 V battery.

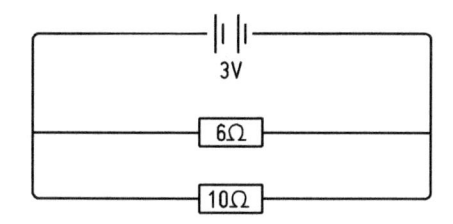

Answer:
Current in the 6 Ω resistor:

$$I = \frac{V}{R} = \frac{3}{6} \; 0.5 \text{ A}$$

Current in the 10 Ω resistor:

$$I = \frac{V}{R} = \frac{3}{10} = 0.33 \text{ A}$$

Current through the 3 V battery:

0.5 A + 0.33 A = 0.83 A

4) Look at the parallel circuit below and calculate the current through the 5 Ω resistor and 10 Ω resistor, then calculate the current through the 12 V battery.

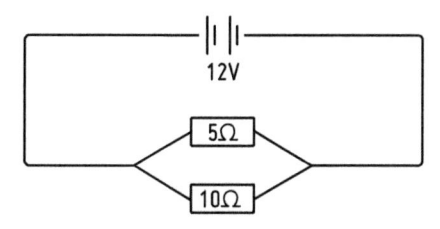

> Note: this is still a parallel circuit; it is just drawn a little differently.

Answer:
Through the 5 Ω resistor:

$$I = \frac{V}{R} = \frac{12}{5} = 2.4 \text{ A}$$

Through the 10 Ω resistor:

$$I = \frac{V}{R} = \frac{12}{10} = 1.2 \text{ A}$$

Total current through the 12 V battery:

2.4 A + 1.2 A = 3.6 A

ENERGY | *Series and parallel circuits*

5) Look at the parallel circuit below. If the current through the 2 Ω resistor is 4 amps, and through the ammeter A is 6 amps, calculate the current through the 4 Ω resistor.

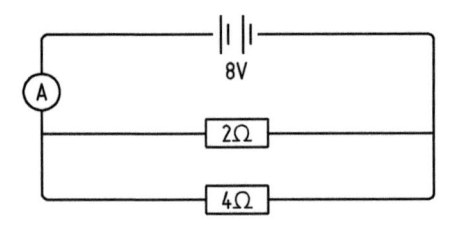

Answer:
The current through A must be the sum of the two branches, i.e. through the 2 Ω and 4 Ω resistors. If it is 6 amps at A and 4 amps through the 2 Ω resistor, then:

6-4 = 2 amps through the 4 Ω resistor.

6)

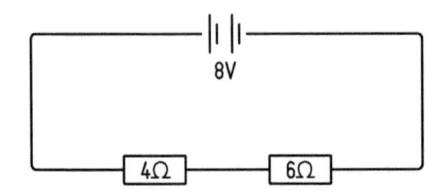

Calculate:
a) the current in the circuit.

b) the voltage across the 4 Ω and 6 Ω resistors.

Answer:
a) current in the circuit.

Total resistance: $R_T = R_1 + R_2$

= 6 + 4

= 10 Ω

Current: $I = \dfrac{V}{R}$

$= \dfrac{8}{10}$

= 0.8 amps

b) Voltage across 4 Ω resistor: V = I × R

   = 0.8 × 4

   = **3.2 volts**

   Voltage across 6 Ω resistor: V = I × R

   = 0.8 × 6

   = **4.8 volts**

   > **Note:** you can check this because the voltage across both resistors should equal to the voltage of the battery, ie: 3.2 V + 4.8 V = 8 V.

Domestic electricity

This section is concerned with electricity in the home and the National Grid.

1) Explain what is meant by AC and DC electricity.

   Answer:
   AC stands for Alternating Current. It is called this because it switches (alternates) direction, constantly reversing. In the UK it reverses direction 50 times a second: this is its frequency. DC stands for Direct Current as it only flows in one direction. Most circuits you will come across at this level will be DC.

2) What is meant by the term 'earthing' and why do we use it on electrical appliances?

   Answer:
   Earthing is a safety feature which stops people being electrocuted by an appliance. It works if a live wire becomes loose and touches the case or handle of a piece of equipment and makes it 'live'. The earth wire in the plug is connected to the ground (earth) outside the building using a metal plate. Any electrical charge will automatically run to ground and 'blow' a fuse in the plug, breaking the circuit and making the device safe.

3) What is a short circuit?

   Answer:
   If the live wire inside an electrical device should touch a neutral wire because it is loose, a current will flow between the two and this is a short circuit. Again, a fuse will blow, shutting off the device.

Electrical power

Power is a measure of how much energy is used per second. Electrical power is specific to the amount of electricity used by an electrical device per second. The unit is the Joule second (J/s) or the watt (W).

$$\text{Power} = \frac{\text{Energy transferred (J)}}{\text{Time taken (s)}}$$

This can be put into a formula triangle:

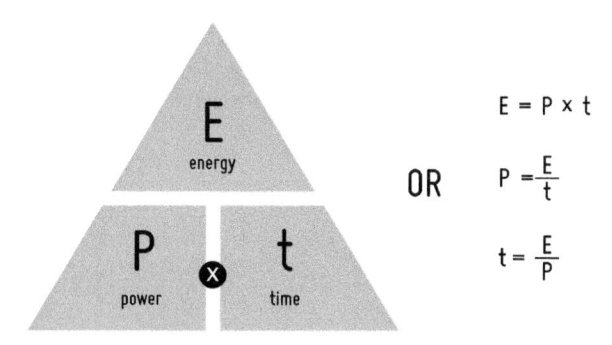

E (energy) / P (power) × t (time)

OR

$E = P \times t$

$P = \frac{E}{t}$

$t = \frac{E}{P}$

Another mathematical relationship to consider is:

power = voltage × current

p = V × I

(p = power, V = voltage, I = current)

and lastly,

p = I²R

This last relationship is often related to a current flowing through a wire or resistor.

> Note: electrical devices use a fuse to protect them. They prevent current flowing by melting if too much flows for a reason like a short circuit or loose connection.

1) A plug contains a fuse for a kettle. The power rating on the kettle is 2500 W (this means it uses 2500 Joules of energy every second to heat water). The kettle is plugged into a standard wall socket of 230 V. Which fuse should be used: 3 A, 5 A, 10 A or 13 A?

> Note: in the UK standard mains voltage for domestic use is 230 V.

Answer:

Power = voltage × current

$p = V \times I$

$I = \dfrac{p}{V}$

$I = \dfrac{2500}{230}$

$= 10.87 \text{ A}$

So a 13 A fuse should be used as the others would 'blow', switching off the circuit.

> **Note:** The fuse chosen for a device should always be of a slightly higher current value than is being used.

2) A microwave oven has a power rating of 800 W. If it is plugged into 230 V from the mains, calculate the size of fuse which should be used. The fuses available are 3 A, 5 A, 7 A and 13 A.

Answer:

$p = V \times I$

$800 = 230 \times I$

$I = \dfrac{800}{230}$

$= 3.47 \text{ A}$

The 5 A fuse should be used.

3) Calculate the power supplied to a 15 A electrical water heater if it is plugged into a 230 V electrical supply.

Answer:

$p = V \times I$

$= 230 \times 15$

$= 3450 \text{ W}$

4) A 120 W camping heater has an electrical resistance of 5 Ω. Calculate the current flowing through the heater.

Answer:
Power = I^2R

120 W = $I^2 \times 5$

$I^2 = \dfrac{120}{5}$

   = 24 A

I = $\sqrt{24}$

   = **4.9 A**

5) A 6 V motor has an electrical resistance of 3 Ω. If it is connected to a 6 V battery, calculate the energy transferred to the motor if it runs for 5 minutes, and the current through the motor.

Answer:
first calculate the current through the motor:

I = $\dfrac{V}{R} = \dfrac{6}{3}$ = **2 A**

next calculate the power of the motor:

P = V × I

P = 6 × 3

P = **18 W**

finally, the energy transferred:

> Note: power is a measure per second, so the time of 5 minutes needs to be converted into seconds!

Power = $\dfrac{energy}{time}$

E = power × time

E = 18 × (5 × 60)

E = 18 × 300

E = **5400 J**

6) An air conditioning unit has a power rating of 7 kw. The cable connecting the unit to the electrical supply warms up slightly. This wire heats up because it has an electrical resistance of 0.15 Ω. The device is supplied with a current of 30 amps. Calculate the energy wasted as heat and the efficiency of the wire.

Answer:
first calculate the mains voltage:

$p = V \times I$

$V = \frac{p}{I}$

$V = \frac{7000}{30}$

$V = 233.3$

next calculate the power supplied:

$p = V \times I$

$p = 233.3 \times 30$

$p = $ **6999 W**

power lost through the cable as heat:

7000 - 6999 = **1 watt**

Efficiency of wire $= \frac{6999}{7000} \times 100$

$= $ **99.98%**

Magnets and electricity

1) Explain the meaning of the following terms:

   a) Magnetic field
   b) Induction magnetism
   c) Pole

   Answer:

   a) A magnetic field is the area or region around a magnet where a force is experienced. This force is greater at the poles of the magnet.

   b) Induction magnetism is when a non-magnetic material becomes 'magnetised', or produced by placing this material in a magnetic field or 'stroking' the material with a magnet.

   c) Poles are the ends of a magnet. One end is a North-seeking pole and the other is the South-seeking pole. They are shortened to North and South.

Magnetism produced by an electric current

1) Describe the shape and the rule used to explain the magnetic field around a current-carrying wire.

Answer:
The magnetic field around a current-carrying wire is in the form of a series of concentric circles around that wire (see diagram A). The field is stronger closer to the wire; also, increasing the current increases the magnetic field strength. The rule used to explain the direction of the field is called the 'right-hand grip rule' (see diagram B).

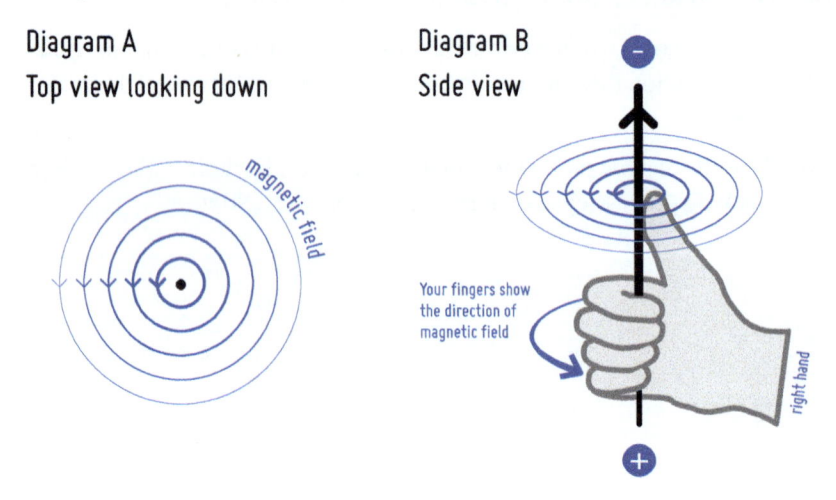

Diagram A
Top view looking down

Diagram B
Side view

Your fingers show the direction of magnetic field

Points to consider:
- Magnetic fields constantly move; they are not static. This is why they may be called 'lines of flux'.
- Electrical current flows from + to − (conventional current).
- The right-hand grip rule works if your thumb points towards the negative terminal, as in the diagram.

2) What is a 'solenoid' and describe the magnetic field around one if the current is flowing.

Answer:
A solenoid is simply a coil of wire. The magnetic field around a solenoid is very similar to the field around a bar magnet. The slight difference is that each line of force is a complete loop in a solenoid because the field passes through the centre of the coil.

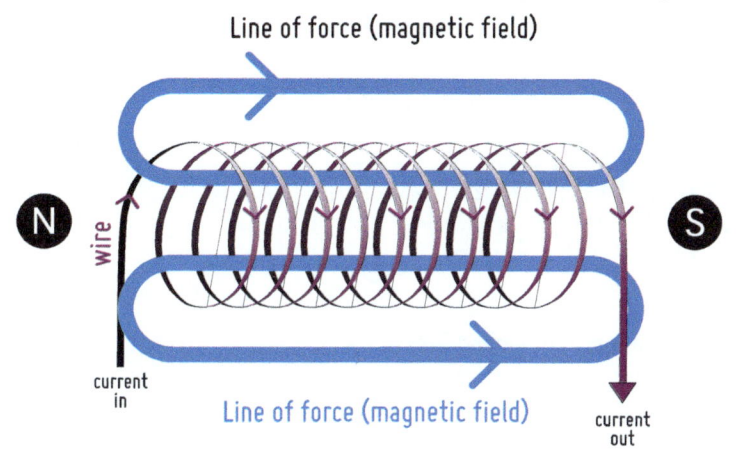

3) Can the magnetic field around a solenoid be made to be stronger?

Answer:
Yes. The strength of the magnetic field can be increased by making the number of coils greater, wrapping the coils tightly close together, increasing the current in the wire, and placing a metal core inside the coil. The core should, however, be made of a metal which can be magnetised, such as iron. The magnetic field, however, dies away when the current is switched off.

4) What is an electromagnet and what are they used for?

Answer:
An electromagnet is a magnet made from a solenoid and an electrical current. The difference is that when the current stops, the magnetic field stops. This gives electromagnets many uses. For example: switches, circuit breakers, relays and scrapyard cranes.

5) What is a circuit breaker and what is it used for?

Answer:
A circuit breaker is a safety device. It is a simple switch which 'breaks' or turns off a circuit if too much electricity flows. The switch is in series with an electromagnet. If too much current flows, the magnetic field increases and pulls the switch open, breaking the circuit. This is often used in the home to protect the many circuits used

and is found on what is called a 'circuit board'. The switch is manually shut after it is broken and the reason for its opening should be investigated.

Low current in wire – low magnetic pull on switch, switch closed, circuit open

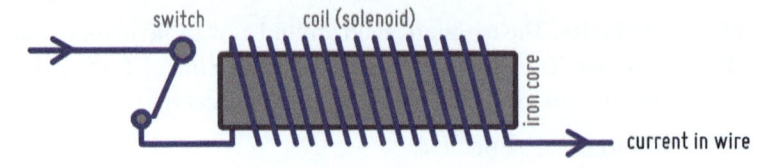

High current in wire – high magnetic pull on switch, switch open, circuit 'broken'

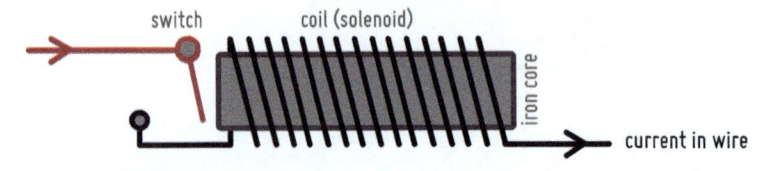

6) a) What is a relay and what are they used for?
   b) How does a relay work?

Answer:
a) A relay is a small electrical circuit and electromagnet which can turn on a larger circuit.

   An example of its use would be a car ignition.

b)

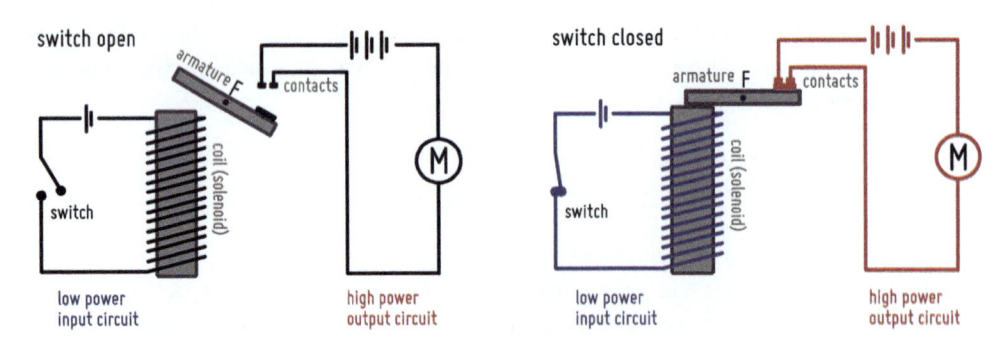

When the switch is closed the solenoid becomes magnetic and attracts the armature downwards towards it. The armature is fixed to a fulcrum 'f' so the bottom half moves to the right, pushing on the contacts closing them. This completes the second circuit, keeping it on. Note the relay circuit must be on at all times for the output circuit to stay on. Think of a car ignition in which the keys have to be left in the on position while the car is in use.

The electric motor

Note: When thinking about the motor effect always look up Fleming's left-hand rule and check you understand it.

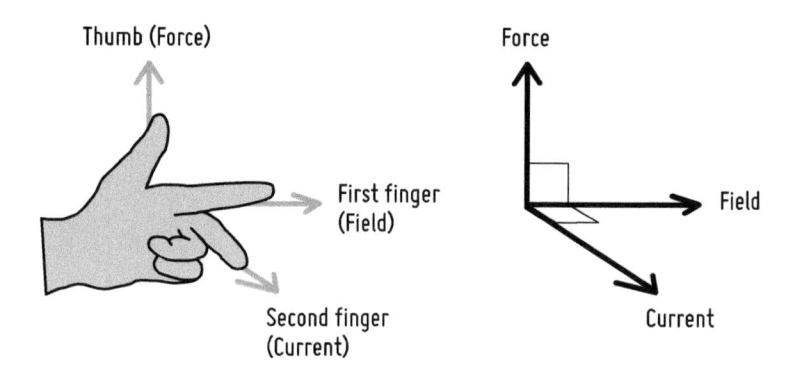

1) What is the motor effect?

   Answer:
   When a current-carrying wire is placed in a magnetic field the wire experiences a force upon it. This force pushes the wire usually out of the field. This is the motor effect. The reason for this is that magnetic lines of force do not like to cross or touch each other, they repel each other. If a current flows through a wire, the wire will have a magnetic field of its own. The two fields, one from the wire the other from the magnet will interact and usually the wire will be pushed out of the magnet's magnetic field.

2) Can the force between two fields be increased or decreased when a current-carrying wire is placed in a magnetic field?

   Answer:
   The simple answer is yes. The force can be increased if the current is increased in the wire because the field around the wire is increased. Increasing the magnetic field from the magnet would also increase the motor effect. Lastly, keeping the wire at 90º or perpendicular to the magnetic field increases the force. If this angle is reduced, so is the force. If the wire becomes parallel to the magnetic field, the force is zero.

3) Consider the diagram below, using Fleming's left-hand rule say if the force is up or down.

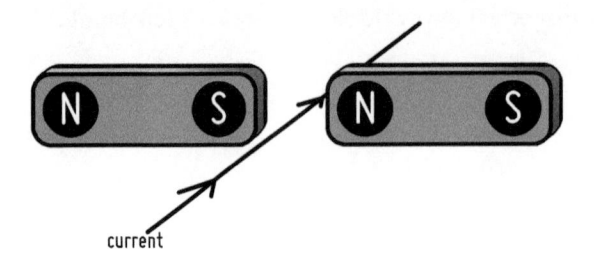

Answer:
Up

4) a) On the diagram below, mark on the direction of the current, magnetic field, force on the wire and the positive and negative sides of the cell.

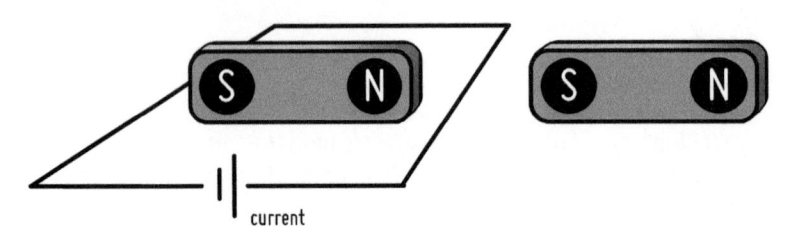

Answer:

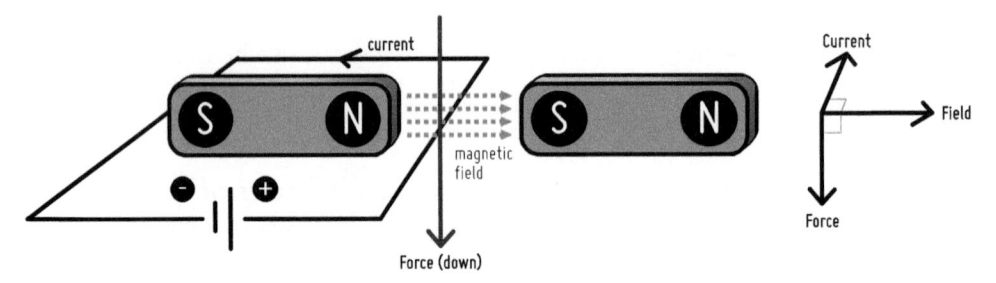

b) What would happen if the current were increased and also if the current were reversed?

Answer:
If the current were increased, then the force would be increased. If the current were reversed, the force would be opposite and would be in an upwards direction.

5) Describe what the term 'magnetic flux density' means and name the equation which links force, current, length and magnetic flux density.

Answer:

Simply put, the magnetic flux density (B) is the strength of a magnetic field. The strength depends upon the length of a conductor carrying a current and the force in a unit area at 90º to the magnetic field. It could be thought of as how many lines of force per unit area. The unit is the 'Tesla'. The equation is:

Force = magnetic flux density × current × length of conductor

F = B × I × L

F = BIL

The units for this equation are:

Force F = Newtons, current I = amperes, length in metres and magnetic flux density = Teslas.

6) Draw a simple diagram of an electric motor and explain how it works. In your explanation say what the commutator, brushes, magnet, coil and spindle do.

Answer:

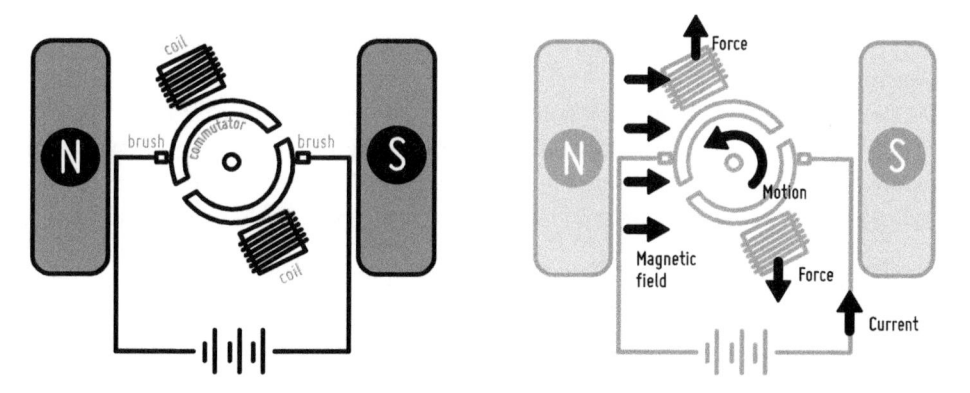

The North and South poles of a magnet face each other with a coil of wire, which can rotate between these two poles. The coil is attached to a spindle in the centre so it can rotate freely. A commutator or split ring is attached to the coil so it also rotates with the coil at the same time. The split ring has two gaps in it, dividing the commutator into two halves. Touching the split ring are two contacts or brushes made of carbon which connect the coil to the battery. When a current flows one side of the coil experiences a force upwards and the other side a downward force. These two opposite forces cause the coil to spin. When the coil is vertical or 90º to the field no lines of force cross or touch, so no force is exerted. The coil is not pushed, but momentum carries the motion on so the coil continues to spin. The coil has swapped sides but the forces produced when the gap has been crossed are produced again in the same direction so the coil continues to spin.

Generators and making electricity from movement and magnetism

> Note: Generators are constructed in a similar way to motors. As the coil of wire rotates in a magnetic field it produces a voltage or potential difference. This process is called 'induction'. If the coil is connected to a complete circuit a current will flow. Making electricity in this way is called the 'generator effect'.

1) What is the difference between an electric motor and a generator?

   Answer:
   Electric motors use electricity to create movement and generators use movement to create electricity.

2) What three things are needed to make electricity using a generator?

   Answer:
   1. Movement. 2. Magnetic field. 3. Current-carrying conductor.

3) A magnet is moved into a coil of wire (solenoid) which is connected to a galvanometer (very sensitive ammeter). Explain what happens to the induced current as the magnet is moved in, out and then held stationary inside the coil.

   Answer:
   As the magnet is moved into the coil the current flows in one direction, say to the right. This is seen as a deflection to the right on the galvanometer. As the magnet is removed the current reverses and flows in the opposite direction (left). If the magnet is held stationary in the coil then no current is induced, so the meter reads zero.

4) Explain how the induced voltage can be increased in a coil of wire.

   Answer:
   There are several ways of increasing the induced voltage or potential difference and therefore the current:

   1. Spin the coil quicker
   2. Increase the strength of the magnetic field
   3. Increase the number of turns in the coil
   4. Increase the area of the coil

Alternators

> **Note:** A simple AC generator (alternator) has two copper slip rings which keep the contacts in constant contact with the circuit. This produces electricity which flows in one direction and then the other, or 'alternates' – hence the name!

1) Draw a current or voltage graph against time and also show the relative positions of the coil as the alternator makes one complete revolution.

Answer:

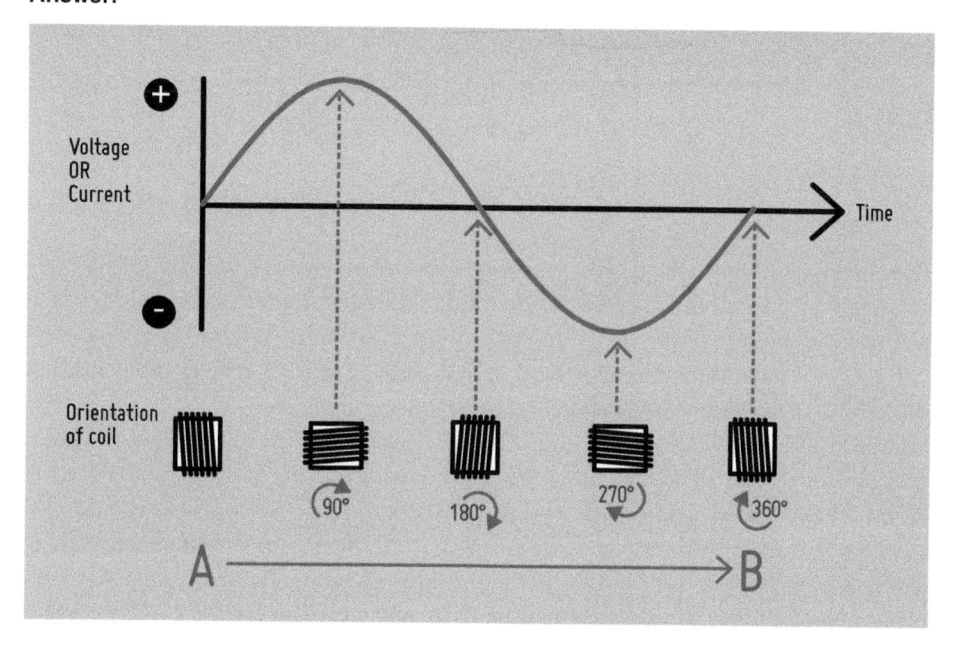

Notice the peak and trough are of equal displacement from rest (height).

Notice the coil has completed one full revolution from A to B.

Transformers

1) Using a diagram, explain how a transformer works and why they only work on AC current.

Answer:

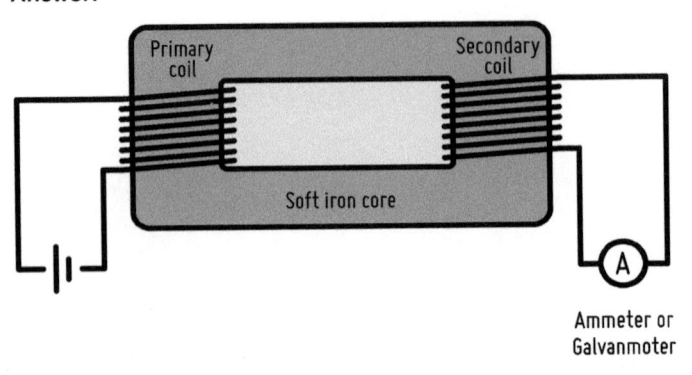

[Diagram: Primary coil and Secondary coil wound around a Soft iron core, primary connected to a battery, secondary connected to an Ammeter or Galvanmoter (A).]

If the primary coil is turned on, a current flows and a magnetic field builds up and sweeps over the coil in the secondary circuit. This sweeping magnetic field 'induces' a current in the secondary coil. If the current in the primary circuit is AC current, it will reach its maximum magnetic field then collapse and then reform in the opposite direction. The constant rise and fall of the magnetic field gives rise to an alternating induced current in the secondary. If a DC (direct current) were used, you would see an initial 'spike' of electricity in the secondary coil, then it would fall back to zero as the magnetic field would be stationary. If the secondary coil has more coils than the primary it will induce a larger voltage and therefore current so it is called a 'stepup' transformer. If the coils are less in number in the secondary, a smaller voltage is produced and this is called a 'step down' transformer. This is called AC mutual induction. The soft iron core increases the magnetic field and the voltage produced and therefore a greater current.

2) Describe the transformer equation used to calculate voltages produced.

Answer:

$$\frac{Voltage\ primary\ (V_p)}{Voltage\ secondary\ (V_s)} = \frac{Number\ turns\ on\ primary\ (N_p)}{Number\ turns\ on\ secondary\ (N_s)}$$

Symbol equation: $\frac{V_p}{V_s} = \frac{N_p}{N_s}$

Or: $\frac{Input\ voltage}{Output\ voltage} = \frac{Turns\ on\ input\ coil}{Turns\ on\ output\ coil}$

3) Complete the following table relating to two different transformers:

	Primary voltage	Secondary voltage	Turns on primary	Turns on secondary
Transformer 1	230 V		2500	150
Transformer 2	20,000	120,000	800	

Answer:

Transformer 1

$$\frac{V_p}{V_s} = \frac{N_p}{N_s}$$

$$\frac{230}{V_s} = \frac{2500}{150}$$

$$\frac{230}{V_s} = 16.66$$

$$V_s = \frac{230}{16.66}$$

$$= \mathbf{13.86 \ V}$$

Because the voltage on the secondary (13.8 V) is less than on the primary, it is a 'step down transformer (voltage is reduced).

Transformer 2:

$$\frac{V_p}{V_s} = \frac{N_p}{N_s}$$

$$\frac{20,000}{120,000} = \frac{800}{N_s}$$

$$0.16 = \frac{800}{N_s}$$

$$N_s = \frac{800}{0.16}$$

$$= \mathbf{5000 \ turns}$$

Current and power in transformers

The equation we use is:

Primary Voltage × Primary Current = Secondary Voltage × Secondary Current

Or

$V_p \times I_p = V_s \times I_s$

> Note: Transformers are very efficient, up to 99%. This is because there are no moving parts. Energy is lost, however, through heating effects due to electrical resistance in the coils. Heat is also lost in the core due to magnetic field changes producing 'eddy currents'. This can be reduced by laminating the core (making it out of layers, not a single piece of soft iron).

4) A step down transformer is used for a laptop computer, changing the mains voltage from 230 V to 19 V. If the laptop runs on 2.3 amps, what is the current in the primary coil to run this device?

Answer:

$V_p \times I_p = V_s \times I_s$

$230 \times I_p = 19 \times 2.3$

$I_p = \dfrac{19 \times 2.3}{230} = \dfrac{43.7}{230}$

= 0.19 amps

5) What is the National Grid?

Answer:
The National Grid is a UK-wide network of power lines and transformers which delivers electricity to consumers, i.e. the public. When electricity flows in a wire, because of electrical resistance some of the electrical energy is lost as heat. To reduce this loss in energy (line loss), transformers are used. A small current is transmitted at a very high voltage which reduces the heat produced and therefore lost electricity. This is achieved by using a step-up transformer. The voltage used can be as high as 400,000 volts when long distances are involved. Once the electricity has reached its intended destination the voltage is reduced to a mains supply domestically of 230 V. This is done using a step down transformer. Reducing the voltage to 230 V is done because 400,000 V would be far too dangerous to us in the home etc. Many devices like laptop computers have a small further step down transformer which reduces the 230 V down to 19 V. This method of electricity distribution is much cheaper than using low voltages and high currents, as the amount of energy loss is estimated to be in the order of 90% using high currents!

Short revision questions on some aspects of electricity and electromagnetism

1) When a material 'x' is rubbed with a silk cloth, explain why it becomes charged positive.

2) Calculate the flow of charge in a circuit if 1.2 amps flow for 3 ½ minutes.

3) What is the current through a device if 63 coulombs flow for 5 minutes?

4) State in words what Ohm's law is.

5) In a circuit 1.3 amps flow through a device with a voltage of 6 V. Calculate the resistance of this circuit.

6) Draw the circuit symbol for a diode and a typical current voltage graph for a diode.

7) For the circuit below calculate the current through the battery:

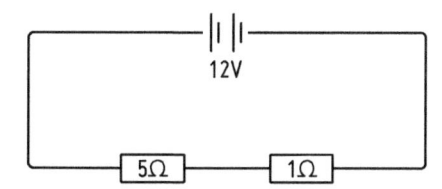

[Circuit diagram: 12V battery with 5Ω and 1Ω resistors in series]

8) For the parallel circuit below calculate the current through the battery:

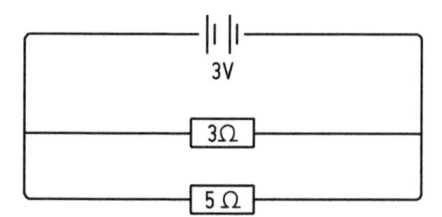

[Circuit diagram: 3V battery with 3Ω and 5Ω resistors in parallel]

9) A vacuum cleaner has a power rating of 500 W, and it is plugged into a mains voltage of 230 V. Which fuse should be used: 2A, 3A or 5A?

10) What is a magnetic field?

11) In the diagram below, which way does the wire move: up or down?

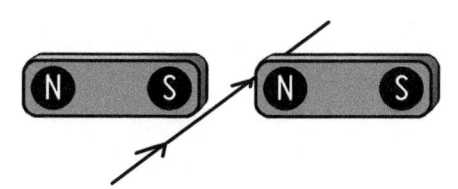

[Diagram showing two magnets (N-S and N-S) with a wire between them]

12) How many turns are on the secondary coil of a transformer if the input voltage is 15,000 volts, output voltage is 95,000 V and the number of turns on the primary coil is 750?

56 WORKSPACE FOR SELF-TESTING

Answers:

1) Friction causes static charges on insulators. The material 'x' has become positive because electrons (negative charges) have left material x and become attached to the cloth. There are more positive charges on the material x now.

2) 252 coulombs.

3) 0.21 amps.

4) Current is proportional to voltage provided the temperature remains constant.

5) 4.62 ohms.

6) see diagrams in the text

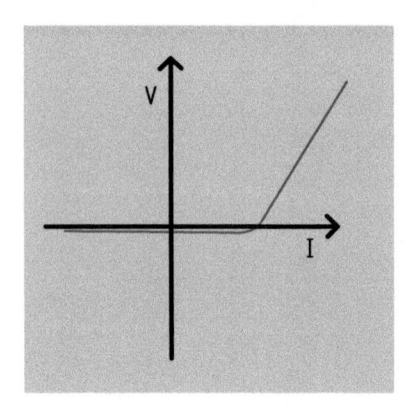

7) 2 amps.

8) 1.6 amps.

9) 3A fuse.

10) A region of space around a magnet where a force is experienced.

11) Up.

12) 4750 turns.

RADIOACTIVITY AND MATTER

Radioactivity and matter

1) Describe the nuclear model of the atom and use a diagram to explain your answer.

   Answer:
   At the centre of the atom is a nucleus which contains two particles: protons and neutrons. Protons have a positive charge and neutrons have no charge, i.e. neutral. Surrounding the nucleus are electrons which have a negative charge. They are arranged in 'orbits' or 'electron shells'. The forces of electrostatic attraction keep the electrons in orbit as they are attracted to the positive nucleus. Note: electrons are constantly moving and it is a 3D model.

   Diagram of the nuclear model of an atom:

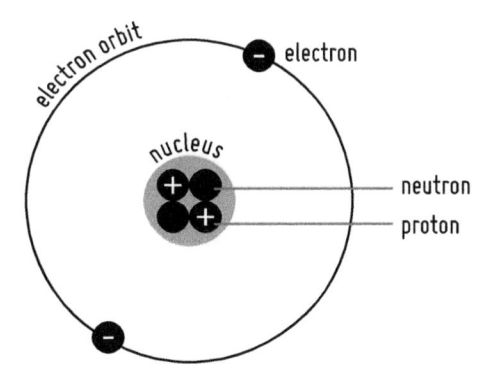

2) Describe the three types of radiation.

   Answer:
   Alpha (α) radiation
   Alpha radiation is a helium nucleus consisting of two protons and two neutrons. The alpha particle has a positive charge, is relatively large and heavy, and is very ionising compared to beta and gamma radiation. Ionising means when the alpha particle crashes into other atoms it knocks off electrons leaving those atoms with a charge and they are now called ions. Because they are quite large they are stopped by thick sheets of paper, skin, or even a few centimetres of air. We say alpha particles are not very

penetrating through materials. Because they are charged they can be bent by magnetic and electric fields.

Beta (β) radiation
Beta particles are fast-moving, high-energy electrons. They move at almost the speed of light. They have almost no mass and are only slightly ionising. They can be stopped by about ½ cm of aluminium or thick card. They have a negative charge so they are also affected by electric and magnetic fields. They are greatly affected by these fields because they have such little mass.

Gamma (γ) radiation
These are waves similar to x-rays; they have no charge or mass. Gamma radiation is only very slightly ionising. Because they have no mass they are very penetrating and are not fully absorbed, even by thick lead. Because they have no charge they are not affected by electric or magnetic fields.

3) Describe the Rutherford, Marsden and Geiger experiment which led to the theory of the 'Nuclear Model' of the atom and discounted the 'Plum Pudding Model'.

Answer:
A radium alpha source was placed in a vacuum along with a thin sheet of gold foil. The alpha particles were directed towards the gold foil and any particles emerging from the gold foil were detected as flashes of light called 'scintillations' on a glass screen coated in zinc sulphide (see diagram below).

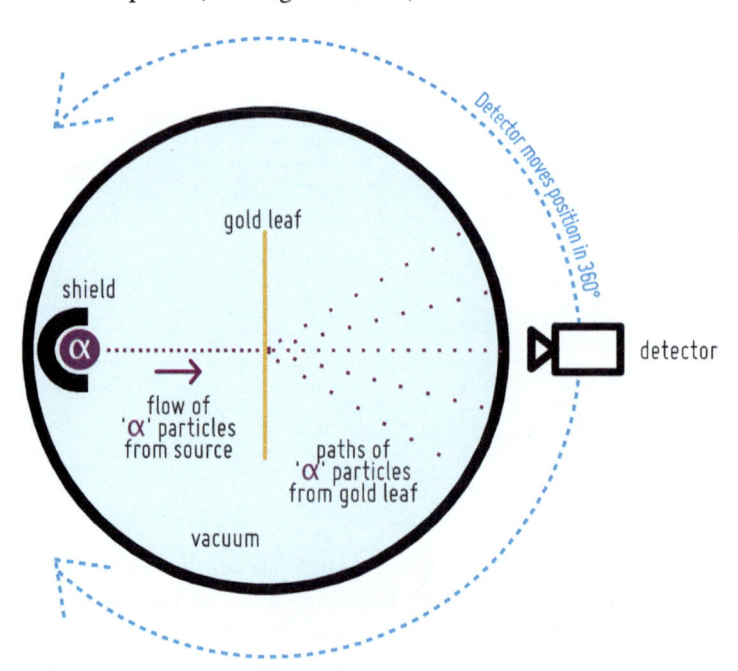

Geiger and Marsden found that most of the alpha particles passed straight through the foil. This showed that atoms are mostly empty space. A very small amount of particles were deflected at an angle of 90° or more. This was an average of about 1 particle in 7500–8000 particles. The number of scintillations decreased with angle. Rutherford concluded the atom had a very small centre of mass which he called the 'nucleus'. He also concluded that the nucleus had a positive charge and the nucleus was tiny. The idea that it had a positive charge came from the fact that alpha particles were repelled by the nucleus and very strongly if they came close to the nucleus itself. Rutherford also believed the nucleus also had another particle inside it which was confirmed in 1932 by James Chadwick. These other particles were called neutrons because they had no charge, while the positive charges were on particles called protons. The modern atomic model was discovered in 1914; before this, scientists described atoms through the 'plum pudding' model. This model suggested the atom had positive and negative charges spread randomly throughout the atom. It did not allow for a nucleus or electron orbits.

> **Note: I always explain that a plum pudding is a Christmas pudding because people don't tend to eat plum puddings these days and students are confused by this!**

4) Describe what we mean by the following terms:
   a) Atomic mass
   b) Atomic number
   c) Isotopes

   Answer:
   a) The atomic mass is the total number (sum) of protons and neutrons in an atom.

   b) The atomic number is the number of protons only in an atom.

   c) Isotopes are different forms of the same atom (nuclide). They have the same atomic numbers, as they have the same number of protons. They have, however, different atomic masses because they have different numbers of neutrons.

5) What are radioactive decay and parent, daughter and decay products?

   Answer:
   When unstable nuclei break up, we call this radioactive decay. When decay happens, alpha (α), beta (β) and gamma (γ) radiations are emitted. New materials are often produced because the atomic number changes.

   Parent atoms are unstable atoms which are about to decay.

   Daughter products are the fragments produced by decay.

   Decay products refer to all the materials and particles produced by decay.

   > **Note: Alpha decay is when a helium nucleus is produced through decay. Its symbol is [$^{4}_{2}\alpha$]**

Hint: you will need a periodic table for these questions

6) What are the decay products when a uranium atom decays by alpha decay? (atomic number 92 and atomic mass 238)

Answer:

$$^{238}_{92}U \rightarrow {}^{4}_{2}\alpha + {}^{234}_{90}Th$$

(uranium → alpha particle + thorium)

7) What is the product of alpha decay from radium (atomic number 88 and mass number 138)?

Answer:

$$^{138}_{88}Ra \rightarrow {}^{4}_{2}\alpha + {}^{134}_{86}Ra$$

(radium → alpha particle + radon)

> Note: With alpha decay, the atomic mass decreases by 4, and the atomic number decreases by 2. This is because an alpha particle is ejected from the atom which has a [$^{4}_{2}\alpha$] make-up. The element changes because the atomic number has changed.

Beta decay

During beta decay a neutron breaks up to produce a new proton and an extra electron. This means the atomic mass of the atom stays the same but the atomic number increases by 1. Note a tiny particle called an 'antineutrino' is also produced but it has almost no mass. We can ignore this at GCSE.

8) What are the decay products if sodium 24 decays by beta decay?

Answer:

$$^{24}_{11}Na \rightarrow {}^{24}_{12}Mg + {}^{0}_{-1}\beta$$

9) What are the decay products if an iodine 131 atom decays by beta decay?

Answer:

$$^{131}_{53}I \rightarrow {}^{131}_{54}Xe + {}^{0}_{-1}\beta$$

10) Explain what gamma radiation (γ) is and why it is usually produced when a nuclide decays through alpha or beta decay. (Nuclide is just a word meaning radioactive material.)

Answer:
When radioactive decay occurs, the protons and neutrons are in an excited state with more than the normal amounts of energy. As these particles rearrange themselves in the atom they lose energy which is then emitted as a 'photon' of gamma radiation. Because photons are pure energy they have no mass or charge. Gamma radiation therefore has no effect upon the atomic number or atomic mass, as there is no mass change. Also it is not affected by electronic or magnetic fields as there is no charge.

11) What is meant by the term 'half-life' (t ½), and use a decay curve to support your answer.

Answer:
Half-life is the time taken for half the atoms in a radioactive substance to decay. Note this is a totally random process as it is impossible to predict which atom will decay and when. A decay curve can be used to work out the average time it takes for half the atoms in a radioactive substance to decay.

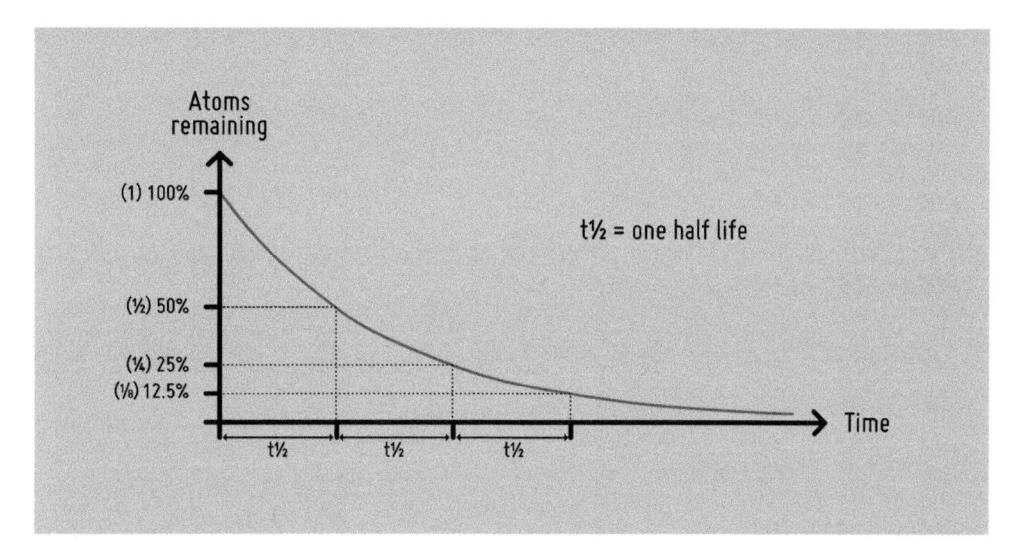

When 50%, i.e. ½, of the atoms decay we call this time t ½ When the number drops by another half of the remaining atoms to 25%, i.e. ¼ of the original number, this takes two half-lives, i.e. 2 × t ½ . When the number drops by half again to ⅛ or 12.5% it takes 3 × t ½ (three half-lives).

> **Note: Common error** – students often think if the atoms decay by say ¼ then this would take 4 half-lives, or by ⅛ of atoms remaining it would take 8 half-lives. This is wrong! It would be true if the line were straight and it was a direct relationship between time and atoms remaining.

12) Radioactive isotope x has a half-life of 20 hours. If the original mass of isotope x is 80 g in a lead container, how much of x will be left after 60 hours?

Answer:
60 hours corresponds to 3 half-lives or ⅛ of atoms remaining so:

$$\frac{80}{8} = 10g$$

Or:

100% of atoms = 80 g (time zero)

50% (½) of atoms = 40 g

25% (¼) of atoms = 20 g

13.5% (⅛) of atoms = **10 g**

13) Radioactive radon 222 has a half-life of 4 days. If the sample mass has a mass of 200 g, how much will be left after 4 half-lives?

Answer:
4 half-lives = $\frac{1}{16}$ of original amount

→ $\frac{200}{16} = 12.5\,g$

14) Radon 222 has a half-life of 4 days. It is an alpha emitter and is used to treat cancerous tumours.

How much time must pass for its activity to fall to $\frac{1}{32}$ of its original value and be totally safe in the body?

Answer:
$\frac{1}{32}$ corresponds to 5 half-lives

4 days × 5 = **20 days**

15) Briefly describe how radiation can be used to check the thickness of materials.

Answer:
For this activity beta (β) particles are used because alpha (α) is too easily stopped and gamma (γ) is too penetrating, and very small differences if any would be detected. A beta source is placed opposite a detector. The materials to be checked are moved between the source and detector. The amount of radiation passing through a material is monitored. If the amount increases the material is becoming thinner, and if the amount of radiation detected decreases the material is becoming thicker. This is used in rolling mills making paper or aluminium foil, for example.

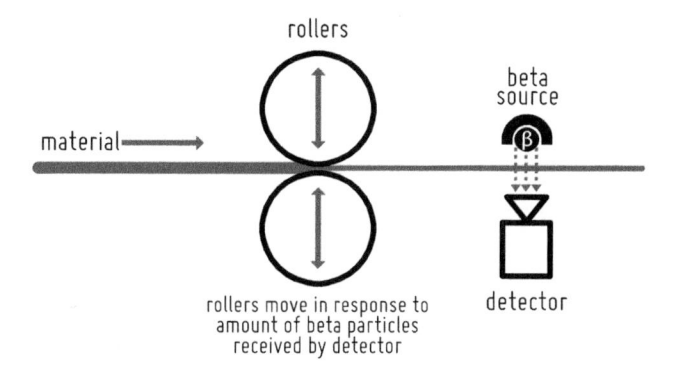

16) How are radioactive tracers used in medicine?

Answer:
Sometimes a patient will swallow or be injected with a radioactive source, usually a beta source. Beta is used because it can escape from the body and be detected and measured. If, for example, a kidney needs to be studied a tracer will be introduced through an intravenous (IV) line in your hand. The liquid will pass through the kidneys after a short while. The radioactive tracer will pass through the kidney and the amount of radioactivity will be detected and converted into an image on a computer. The patient will then be asked to drink lots of water to 'flush' the tracer from their system. Soft tissue organs in the kidney or liver can't be x-rayed like bones as they don't stop x-rays and nothing will be seen.

17) What is nuclear fission?

Answer:
Nuclear fission is a fast nuclear reaction which uses neutrons to smash unstable atoms apart. Uranium is used in nuclear power stations to produce heat. Neutrons are fired at uranium atoms. If a neutron hits a uranium atom it may split up into roughly two equal halves. It will also release two or three other neutrons. These neutrons recently released from an atom will fly off at great speed and collide with other uranium atoms, and so on. With each collision energy is also released and this quickly escalates. This is known as a 'chain reaction'. If left unchecked, it could release huge amounts of energy

quickly as a nuclear explosion. In power stations this reaction is controlled by fuel rods and a moderator so the energy released is constant and controllable. The classic diagram to go with this question can be seen below.

A chain reaction:

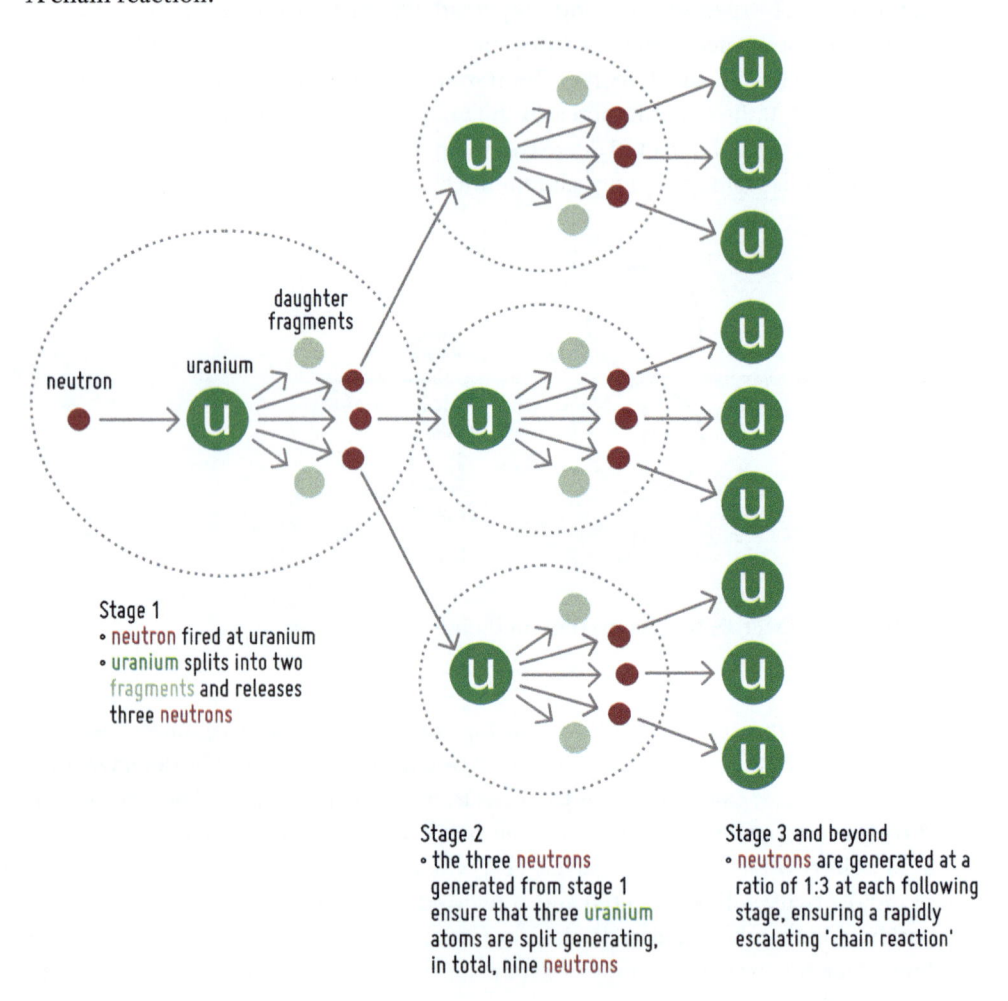

Stage 1
- **neutron** fired at uranium
- **uranium** splits into two **fragments** and releases three **neutrons**

Stage 2
- the three **neutrons** generated from stage 1 ensure that three **uranium** atoms are split generating, in total, nine **neutrons**

Stage 3 and beyond
- **neutrons** are generated at a ratio of 1:3 at each following stage, ensuring a rapidly escalating 'chain reaction'

18) What is nuclear fusion and where does it occur?

Answer:
Nuclear fusion is the opposite to fission. It is the joining of two light elements (hydrogen) to make a new, heavier element and in doing so release huge amounts of energy. This type of reaction happens in stars like our Sun and has been used in the 'hydrogen bomb' in World War Two. It is called fusion because the atoms 'fuse' together to make a new element. Weight for weight, nuclear fusion produces much more energy than fission, reaching temperatures and atomic speeds of vast amounts. The atoms must travel at colossal speeds as when they crash and fuse together they have to overcome the forces of repulsion trying to keep the atoms apart. Nuclear

fusion can be explained by the reaction between tritium (hydrogen 3) and deuterium (hydrogen 2).

Two isotopes of hydrogen (tritium and deuterium) are forced together to produce helium and a neutron.

$$_{1}^{2}H \; _{1}^{3}H \rightarrow \; _{2}^{4}He + _{0}^{1}n$$

(Deuterium) + (tritium) → (helium) + (neutron)

19) Describe how a nuclear reactor works. Include in your answer what we mean by the terms moderator, control rods and fuel rods.

> **Note: Before you consider this answer I always explain to my students that 'all fossil fuels or nuclear power stations are like giant kettles. They boil water to make steam, which drive turbines which drive generators to make electricity.'**

Answer:

Nuclear power stations use fission reactions (splitting up atoms) to release heat energy. Typically, they use uranium-235. The fuel rods contain uranium dioxide which is natural uranium ore enriched with the isotope uranium-235 (2–5%). The uranium-235 is in low concentration because if it were too high a concentration, the chain reaction would be difficult to control. The graphite core is called the moderator, which slows down the neutrons released by the reaction. The moderators are placed in rows with the fuel rods (see diagram).

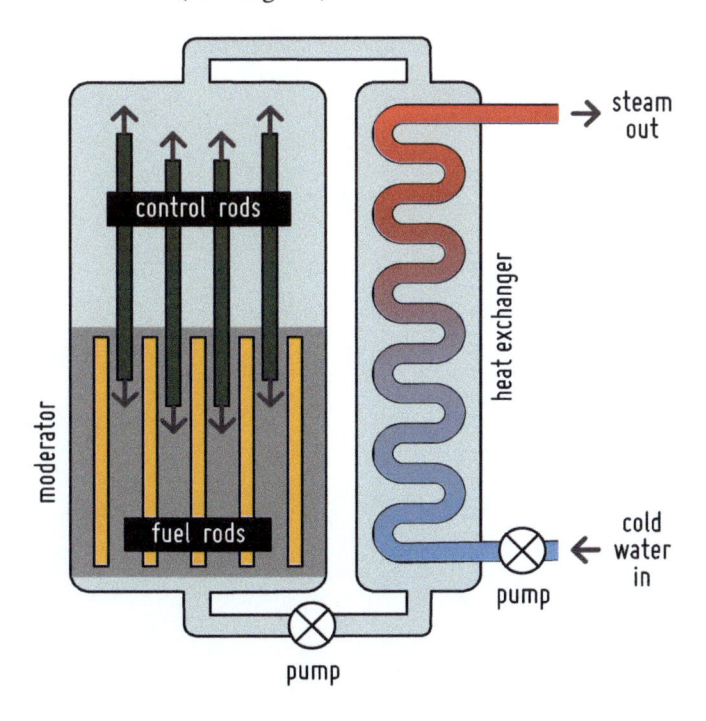

The neutrons are slowed down because if they are moving too fast they have less chance of colliding with uranium atoms. The control rods are made of boron as this also absorbs neutrons. The control rods are lowered between the fuel rods and the moderators to absorb neutrons. The whole design is designed to control the amount and speed of neutrons released, and therefore the pace and amount of energy released.

As the control rods are lowered between the moderator and fuel rods more neutrons are absorbed, therefore slowing the reaction. The reaction can be completely stopped by lowering the rods fully down. The fuel (uranium) does get used up and some of it turns into plutonium- 239, which has to be periodically removed from the reactor.

The heat produced by the reaction is removed either by pressurised water or by carbon dioxide gas which surrounds the reactor vessel. The whole reactor is cased in thick concrete to stop radiation leaks. The hot water/gases are then moved over a heat exchanger to make superheated steam to drive a turbine.

Short revision questions on radioactivity

1) Describe the nuclear model of the atom. Include in your answer the words: proton, neutron, nucleus, electron, electron orbit.

2) Using a diagram of gold atoms, explain the conclusions to the Rutherford, Marsden and Geiger experiment.

3) Complete the following **alpha** decay equations:

   a) $^{235}_{92}U \rightarrow$

   b) $^{226}_{88}Ra \rightarrow$

   c) $^{216}_{84}Po \rightarrow$

4) Complete the following **beta** decay equations:

   a) $^{14}_{6}C \rightarrow$

   b) $^{216}_{84}Po \rightarrow$

   c) $^{87}_{37}Rb \rightarrow$

5) A radioactive substance has a half-life of one hour. What percentage of atoms will not have decayed after two hours?

6) An isotope of neon has an initial count rate of 1000 counts per minute. This reduces to 125 counts per minute in 6 hours. How long is the half-life of this isotope?

7) A radon isotope has an initial count rate of 836 counts per minute. Calculate the counts per minute after:

   a) One half-life
   b) Two half-lives
   c) Four half-lives

70 WORKSPACE FOR SELF-TESTING

WORKSPACE FOR SELF-TESTING

Answers:

1) See first question in this section.

2) i)   atom mostly empty space

   ii) nucleus has positive charge

   iii) nucleus is tiny

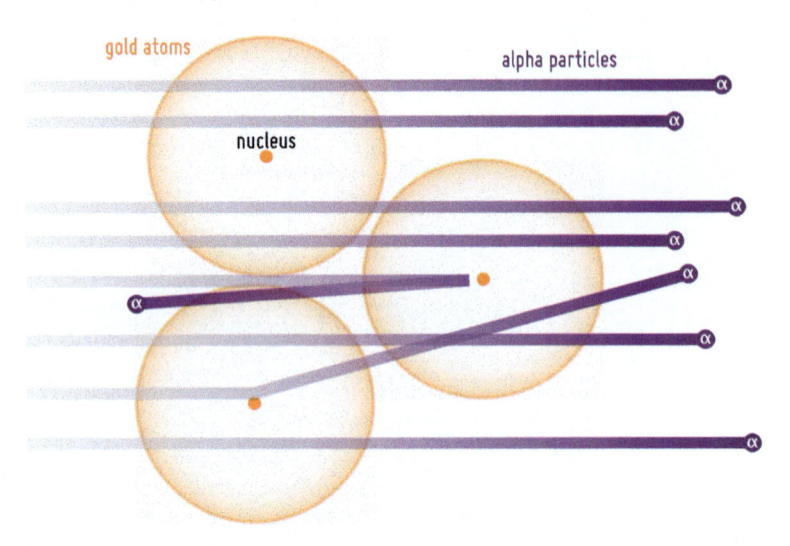

3) a) $^{235}_{92}U \rightarrow \, ^{4}_{2}\alpha + \, ^{231}_{90}Th$

   b) $^{226}_{88}Ra \rightarrow \, ^{4}_{2}\alpha + \, ^{222}_{86}Rn$

   c) $^{216}_{84}Po \rightarrow \, ^{4}_{2}\alpha + \, ^{212}_{82}Pb$

4) a) $^{14}_{6}C \rightarrow \, ^{14}_{7}N + \, ^{0}_{-1}\beta$

   b) $^{216}_{84}Po \rightarrow \, ^{216}_{85}At + \, ^{0}_{-1}\beta$

   c) $^{87}_{37}Rb \rightarrow \, ^{87}_{38}Sr + \, ^{0}_{-1}\beta$

5) 25% left (because two half-lives passed).

6) Two hours. Because:

$$\frac{1000}{125} = 8$$

so 125 is $\frac{1}{8}$ of 1000

$\frac{1}{8}$ corresponds to three half-lives

$\frac{6}{3}$ = **two hours**

7) a) 50% e.g. $\frac{836}{2}$ = **418 count**

b) 25% e.g. $\frac{836}{4}$ = **209 count**

c) Four half-lives = $\frac{1}{16}$ = $\frac{836}{16}$ = 52.25 or **52 counts**.

MATTER

Density

Density is a measure of how much matter or material in terms of atoms and molecules there are per unit volume. I often tell my students it is the amount of 'stuff' in an object.

For example, 1m³ of lead has a mass of 11,400 kg, whereas 1 m³ of air has a mass of 1.3 kg. This is because there are a lot more lead atoms in 1 m³ of lead than there are atoms and molecules in 1 m³ of air!

To calculate density, we use the formula:

$$density = \frac{mass}{volume}$$

This can be put into the formula triangle:

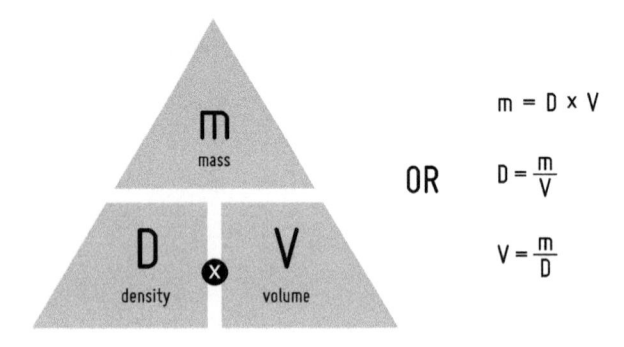

$m = D \times V$

OR

$D = \frac{m}{V}$

$V = \frac{m}{D}$

1) How large should a petrol container be if it needs to hold 50 kg of petrol? (the density of petrol is 800 kg/m³).

   Answer:
   Mass of petrol = 50 kg

   Density of petrol = 800 kg/m³

   $V = \frac{mass}{density} = \frac{50}{800}$

   = 0.0625 m³

2) What is the mass of water required to fill a 1.5 m³ paddling pool? (density of water = 1000 kg/m³)

Answer:

Mass = volume × density

= 1.5 × 1000

= **1500 kg**

3) The density of gold is 19,300 kg/m³. If a gold bar measures 20 cm in length, 5 cm high and 10 cm wide, calculate the mass of the gold bar.

Answer:
Firstly, convert the centimetres into metres:

20 cm = 0.2 m

5 cm = 0.05 m

10 cm = 0.1 m

Secondly, calculate the volume of the gold bar using:

volume = length × height × width

= 0.2 × 0.05 × 0.1

= 0.001 m³

Lastly use the formula: mass = density × volume

M = D × V

M = 19,300 × 0.001

M = **19.3 kg.**

4) Calculate the mass of a granite block and block of ice, both with a volume of 1.5 m³. The density of granite is 2700 kg/m³ and ice at 0°C is 920 kg/m³.

Answer:
In both cases we use: mass = density × volume

Granite = 2700 × 1.5

= **4050 kg.**

Ice = 920 × 1.5

= **1380 kg.**

5) A drop of mercury has a mass of 0.544 g. The volume of the drop is 0.04 cm³. Using this information, calculate the density of mercury.

Answer:

Density $= \dfrac{M}{V}$

$= \dfrac{0.544}{0.04}$

Density $= 13.6 \text{ g/cm}^3$.

6) Calculate the density of lead using the following information: A lead toy soldier has a mass of 72 g and a volume of 6.31 cm³.

Answer:

Density $= \dfrac{M}{V}$

$= \dfrac{72}{6.31}$

Density $= 11.41 \text{ g/cm}^3$.

The Gas Laws

Gases are much more complicated than solids and liquids in terms of their behaviour. This is because of the random nature of their movement and the fact they are easily squashed or compressed. If we change either the temperature, volume or pressure of a gas it will affect the conditions of either one or both of the other two factors.

Boyle's Law

"for a fixed mass of gas, at constant temperature, P × V is a constant" (P = pressure and V = volume)

When doing experiments on gases we find:

If the pressure is doubled the volume is halved, and if the pressure is trebled the volume is reduced to one third of the initial volume.

This means that:

the volume of a gas is inversely proportional to the pressure, which can be expressed as:

$$P \alpha \frac{1}{V}$$

Or, more often Boyle's law is written as:

$$P_1 V_1 = P_2 V_2$$

1) A diver is swimming below the surface of the sea and the pressure on the diver is 3.5 atmospheres. At first a bubble of expelled air measures 3 cm³ in volume. When the bubble reaches the surface of the water the pressure is 1 atmosphere and it pops. Calculate the volume of the bubble just before it popped.

Answer:
Formula: $P_1 V_1 = P_2 V_2$

Underwater P = 3.5 atmos and V = 3 cm³

At the surface P = 1 atmos and V = ?

So $P_1 V_1 = P_2 V_2$

3.5 × 3 = 1 V₂

$V_2 = \dfrac{3.5 \times 3}{1} = \dfrac{10.5}{1}$

= 10.5 cm³

> Note: The bubble has expanded due to the reduction in pressure as it reaches the surface of the water.

2) A balloon is filled with 9.3 litres of gas at a pressure of 3 atmospheres. If the pressure is reduced on the balloon to 0.8 atmospheres, what would the volume of the balloon be now?

Answer:
Formula: $P_1 V_1 = P_2 V_2$

Initial

3 × 9.3 = 0.8 × V₂

$V_2 = \dfrac{3 \times 9.3}{0.8}$

= 34.8 litres

Charles' Law

Charles' Law looks at how temperature effects pressure while keeping the pressure constant. This means the gas can expand or contract freely in a container.

The classic graph to represent the volume against temperature is seen below:

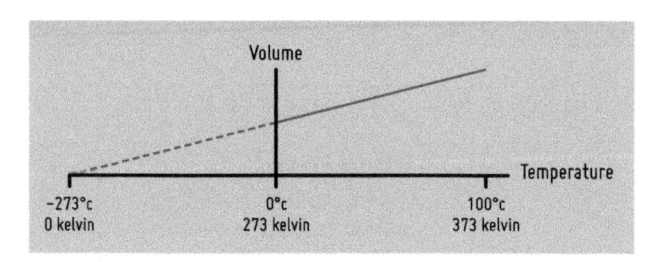

The point at which the line crosses the x axis is at -273°C. This is very important in physics as it represents 'Absolute Zero'. This is the theoretically coldest temperature possible where nearly all molecules stop vibrating. This temperature is also the zero on the 'Kelvin' scale. On the Kelvin scale 0°C is 273 Kelvin. The Kelvin scale goes up in units similar to the Celsius scale but starts at the theoretical point of minus -273°C or zero Kelvin.

Charles' Law

"for a fixed mass of gas, at constant pressure, the volume of the gas is directly proportional to the absolute temperature (T)". (See previous graph)

Mathematically: V α T so V = constant × T

giving $\frac{V}{T}$ = constant ⇒ $\frac{V_1}{T_1} = \frac{V_2}{T_2}$

(Note T is the absolute temperature measured in Kelvin)

> **Hint: when doing Charles' law calculations always convert degrees Celsius into Kelvin.**

Why convert the temperature to Kelvin, I hear you ask!

The reason is that some, if not most, gases exist in the gas state at 0°C. This means when doing calculations the temperature in Celsius could be zero, and since temperature is the denominator in the combined equation of the ideal gas law we would be dividing by zero. This makes no sense as no number multiplied by zero exists!

The combined Charles' law and Boyle's law equations give the ideal gas equation (see below).

$$\frac{PV}{T} = Constant$$

Or:

$$\frac{P_1 V_1}{T_1} = \frac{P_2 V_2}{T_2}$$

1) Calculate the volume of air which is heated to 80°C if its volume at 30°C is 2 m³.

   Use Charles' law relationship

   Answer:
   Note the temperature is converted into Kelvin

   $$\frac{V_1}{T_1} = \frac{V_2}{T_2}$$

   $$= \frac{2m^3}{303K} = \frac{V_2}{353K}$$

   $$= 0.0066 = \frac{V_2}{353}$$

   $$= V_2 = 0.0066 \times 353$$

   $$= 2.32 \text{ m}^3$$

2) How do you convert from Celsius to Kelvin?

   Answer:
   This is a simple operation, see the examples below:
   a) 0°C = 273 Kelvin
   b) 10°C = 273 + 10 = 283 Kelvin
   c) -10°C = 273 - 10 = 263 Kelvin
   d) 100°C = 273 + 100 = 373 Kelvin
   e) -273°C = 0 Kelvin
   f) 25°C = 273 + 25 = 298 Kelvin

3) A 2.5 m³ volume of air is at 26°C. What temperature must the air be raised to so that its volume increases to 3.5 m³? (Note the pressure is constant)

Answer:
(use Charles' law)

$$\frac{V_1}{T_1} = \frac{V_2}{T_2}$$

and convert the temperatures into Kelvin

$$\frac{2.5m^3}{299K} = \frac{3.5m^3}{T_2}$$

$$= 0.00836 = \frac{3.5}{T_2}$$

$$T_2 = \frac{3.5}{0.00836}$$

$$= \mathbf{418.66\ K}\ (\text{or } 145.6°C)$$

The combined gas equation

We can combine Boyle's law (PV = constant) and Charles' law (V/T = constant) and the pressure law (P/T= constant) to give the combined gas equation:

$$\frac{PV}{T} = constant$$

Which can be rearranged to:

$$\frac{P_1 V_1}{T_1} = \frac{P_2 V_2}{T_2}$$

(again the temperature in Kelvin)

> Hint: because there are 6 terms in the combined gas equation, always list the terms you know first and remember the temperature is in Kelvin.

4) A bicycle pump with the handle out contains 60 cm³ of air at normal atmospheric pressure of 1 atmosphere. The temperature of the air in the pump is 10°C. The plunger is pushed down and the air is compressed to 20 cm³. The temperature of the air in the pump increases to 32°C.

   Calculate the pressure in the gas now.

   Answer:
   First write the formula to be used:

   $$\frac{P_1 V_1}{T_1} = \frac{P_2 V_2}{T_2}$$

   Next list all the terms you know:

   P_1 = 1 atmosphere

   V_1 = 60 cm³

   T_1 = 10°C + 273 = 283 K

   P_2 = ?

   V_2 = 20 cm³

   T_2 = 32°C + 273 = 305 K

   Next substitute in the terms:

   $$\frac{1 \times 60}{283} = \frac{P_2 \times 20}{305}$$

   This is clearly not straightforward to solve so we need to make P_2 the subject of the equation (see below).

   Combined gas law:

   $$\frac{P_1 V_1}{T_1} = \frac{P_2 V_2}{T_2}$$

Step 1: cross multiplying gives -

$P_1 \times V_1 \times T_2 = T_1 \times P_2 \times V_2$

Step 2: To get rid of T_1 and V_2 to leave P_2 which we are trying to find; divide both sides by T_1 and V_2 gives -

$$\frac{P_1 \times V_1 \times T_2}{T_1 \times V_2} = \frac{\cancel{T_1} \times P_2 \times \cancel{V_2}}{\cancel{T_1} \times \cancel{V_2}}$$

Step 3: Cancelling out the T_1 and V_2 on the right-hand side of the equation leaves –

$$\frac{P_1 \times V_1 \times T_2}{T_1 \times V_2} = P_2$$

Step 4: Substitute in the values for each term again –

$$\frac{1 \times 60 \times 305}{283 \times 20} = P_2$$

$$P_2 = \frac{18300}{5660}$$

= **3.23 atmospheres**

Change of state

You should already be familiar with the structure and general properties of solids, liquids and gases. You should also be aware that the change between a solid, liquid and gas requires a change in energy. Important terms are: melting point (MP), boiling point (BP) and freezing point (FP). These are temperatures at which a change of state or phase happens.

Latent heat

The word 'latent' means hidden. In this context it is the energy substances give out or take in during a change of state. When observing this we notice there is no change in temperature. The energy supplied is used to break bonds, molecules or atoms to move position or form new structures such as in freezing.

> Hint: with this topic questions usually focus upon graphs and what they mean (see below) or calculating latent heat or energy supplied.

Typical graphs:

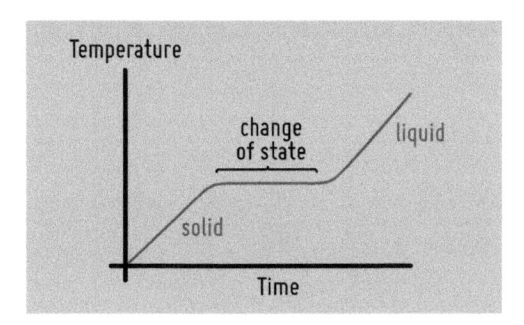

Notice the flat part of the graph is where the change of state happens. The temperature remains constant while a substance changes phase.

1) Draw a graph showing the heating of ice through to its gas phase (state), and on this graph label the melting point (MP), boiling point (BP) and the states of matter.

   Answer:

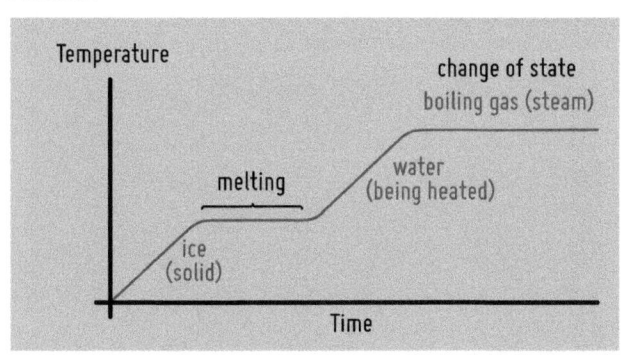

2) What is the difference between boiling and evaporation?

   Answer:
   Evaporation only happens at the surface of a liquid, whereas boiling happens throughout the whole liquid.

Specific latent heat of fusion

This is latent heat but using 1 kg to quantify the amount of energy needed, so scientists can compare values of energy needed to change the state of different materials.

"The specific latent heat of fusion is the amount of energy required to change the state of 1 kg of a substance from a solid to a liquid."

The units for latent heat are Joules, as it is an example of energy transfer.

Formula: E = Energy, SLHF = specific latent heat of fusion, M = mass

$$Lf = \frac{\text{energy supplied}}{\text{mass}}$$

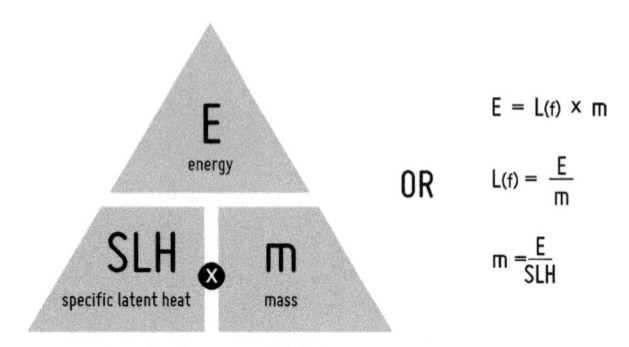

$$E = L_{(f)} \times m$$

OR

$$L_{(f)} = \frac{E}{m}$$

$$m = \frac{E}{SLH}$$

We have for specific latent heat of vaporisation the same formula, but we use Lv for specific latent heat of vaporisation.

> **Note: The units for specific latent heat of fusion or vaporisation are Joules per kilogram, i.e. J/kg.**

1) How much energy is needed to vaporise 12 g of mercury? (Lf of mercury is 11,000 J/kg)

   Answer:
   First convert 12 g into kg which is 0.012 kg.

   $E = Lf \times M$

   $E = 11,000 \times 0.012$

   $E = $ **132 Joules**

2) How much energy is needed to melt 5 kg of ice? (Lf for ice is 334,000 J/kg)

   Answer:
   $E = L_f \times M$

   $E = 334,000 \times 5$

   $E = $ **1.67 $\times 10^6$ Joules**

3) A pan of water is boiling on an electric hob for 110 seconds. Over this period of time 150 g water is lost as steam. The power rating of the hob is 3500 watts. Calculate the specific latent heat of steam, and explain why your answer is greater than the actual figure of 2,300,000 J/kg for steam.

Answer:
First convert the 150 g to kg, as the answer asks for specific latent heat which is kg.

So, 150 g = **0.15 kg**.

Next note 3500 watts is 3500 Joules per second so we need to calculate the energy used in 110 seconds:

3500 × 110 = **385,000 Joules**.

$$S_v = \frac{E}{M} = \frac{385{,}000}{0.15}$$

= **2,566,666.7 Joules OR 2567 kJ/kg**

Note: S_v = SLH of vaporisation.

The answer is larger than the actual figure because the pan is not insulated so heat energy is wasted heating up the pan itself and the surroundings.

Short revision questions on density, gas laws and change of state

1) A stone has a mass of 28 g and is dropped into a measuring cylinder with 60 cm³ of water in it. The water rises to 80 cm³. Calculate the density of the stone.

2) A balloon is inflated for a party with air, to a volume of 0.015 m³. Air has a density of 1.3 kg/m³. Calculate the mass of air in the balloon.

3) Convert the following temperatures from degrees Celsius to Kelvin:

   a) 23°C

   b) 105°C

   c) -15°C

   d) -180°C

4) Convert the following temperatures from degrees Kelvin to Celsius:

   a) 310 K

   b) 124 K

   c) 303 K

   d) 287 K

5) Using $P_1 V_1 = P_2 V_2$ solve the following problem:

   Bubbles are escaping from the sea floor at a pressure of 4 atmospheres and are 6 cm in diameter. When the bubbles reach the surface of the sea, which is at 1 atmosphere, calculate the volume of the bubbles now.

6) Using the combined gas equation, solve the following problem:

   An inflatable bath toy contains 25 cm³ of air at 1 atmosphere and is at 10°C. If the toy is then pumped up to its maximum volume of 35 cm³ and the temperature doubles to 20°C, calculate the pressure inside the toy.

7) How much energy is needed to vaporise 10 g of carbon dioxide? The L_f of CO_2 is 574 kJ/kg.

WORKSPACE FOR SELF-TESTING 89

Answers:
1) 1.4 g
2) 0.0195 kg
3) a) 296 K
   b) 378 K
   c) 258 K
4) a) 37°C
   b) -149°C
   c) 30°C
   d) 14°C
5) 24 cm³
6) 1.4 atmospheres
7) 5740 Joules

FORCES

Scalar and vector quantities

> Key point: scalar quantities only have a size whereas a vector quantity has size and direction.

Note: Scientists like to use the word 'magnitude' rather than 'size'.

Examples

Scalar	Vectors
Speed	Acceleration
Distance	Velocity
Time	Weight
Mass	Force
Energy	Momentum

A good way of thinking about this topic is to consider speed and velocity. People will often comment about how fast they are driving, for example:

"I was driving at 70 mph on the M5."

This just tells the person listening how quickly the car was moving, i.e. its speed, but does not indicate where the car was going.

Velocity, however, is very important when we consider ships and aeroplanes, as they use velocity for navigation. Also wind/current speeds and directions need to be calculated, making this sometimes very difficult to calculate. Essentially aeroplanes and ships need to use compass bearings and speeds to navigate as there are no landmarks out at sea or above the clouds. An aeroplane, for example, may take a velocity of 500 km/h North-West for 30 minutes to reach a destination.

Consider the following map:

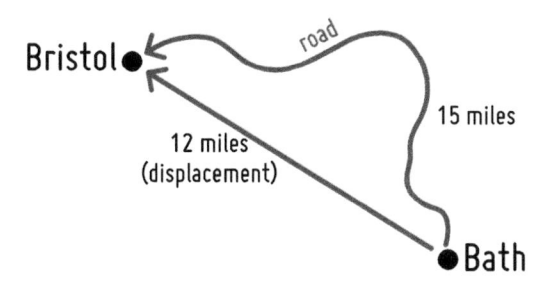

Bristol ← road
12 miles (displacement)
15 miles
● Bath

The displacement between two points is the shortest distance in a straight line. In this example it is 12 miles between Bristol and Bath. The road between the two cities is, however, not straight so the distance travelled is 15 miles. The displacement may be described as 12 miles north-west from Bath.

Arrows can be used to describe or represent forces. The size and direction give the reader an idea of size and direction of the force. (Note: Force is a vector as it has size and direction.)

Examples:

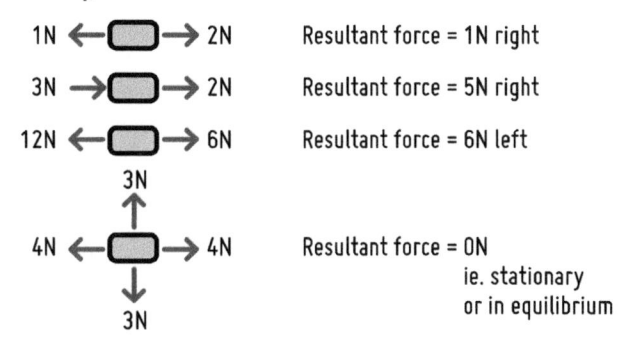

1N ←☐→ 2N   Resultant force = 1N right

3N →☐→ 2N   Resultant force = 5N right

12N ←☐→ 6N   Resultant force = 6N left

```
        3N
        ↑
4N ←☐→ 4N     Resultant force = 0N
        ↓            ie. stationary
        3N           or in equilibrium
```

What happens if forces act at an angle to each other?

Answer:
We can use a process called parallelogram of forces to find the overall effect. We call this the 'resultant'. We could also describe the result as a horizontal and vertical component which we will see later. Essentially we draw a parallelogram, which is a shape with two sides that are parallel to each other.

Consider:

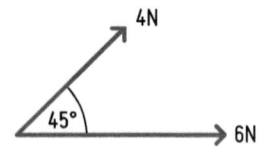

What is the resultant force produced by combing two forces of 4 N and 6 N which are at 45º to each other?

a) choose a suitable scale as the diagram will be drawn accurately to scale, the size of the force and direction indicated by the arrows.

b) In the diagram above use a scale of 1 cm – 1 Newton so the arrows are 4 cm and 6 cm at 45º to each other. Then draw in the other two sides to make a parallelogram, see below:

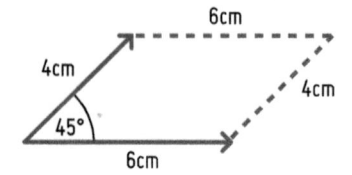

c) Then draw a diagonal line from the original angle of 45º to the opposite corner. This line (or arrow) is the resultant. We then measure this arrow and convert the answer to the force using the scale chosen. We also give it a double arrow, indicating it is the resultant (see next diagram).

Final answer:

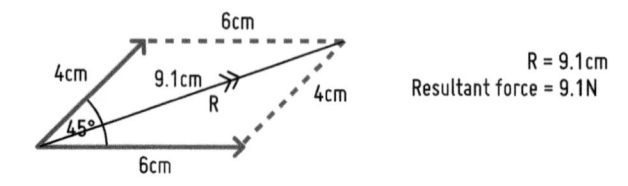

R = 9.1cm
Resultant force = 9.1N

R = 9.1 cm

R = **9.1 Newtons**

1) Two forces act at an angle of 22° to each other. The force in the vertical is 15 N and in the horizontal is 6 N. Calculate the resultant force.

Answer:
Use the scale 1 cm = 1 N

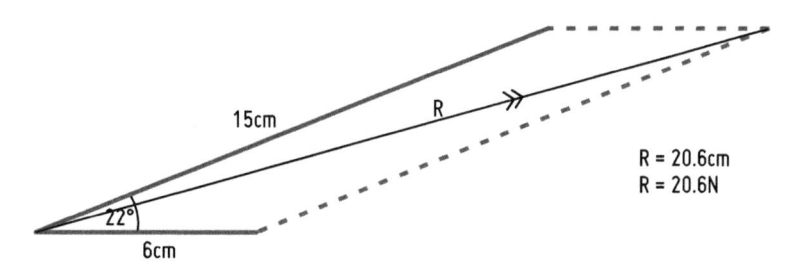

R = 20.6cm
R = 20.6N

You should draw the diagram on graph paper to scale and measure the angle with a protractor.

The diagram gives us:

R = 20.6 cm

R = 20.6 N.

2) Calculate the resultant force if two forces of 50 kN and 80 kN act at 60° to each other.

Answer:
The first thing to do is realise that kN means 1000 Newtons, so 50 kN = 50,000 N and 80 kN = 80,000 N. Next use a scale of 1 cm = 10,000 N.

Diagram (not to scale). You should draw on graph paper yourself to check.

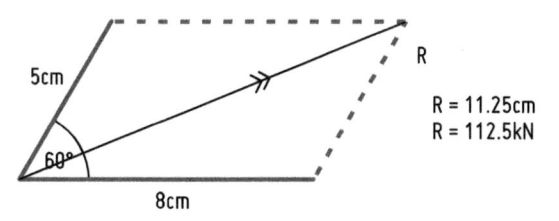

R = 11.25cm
R = 112.5kN

R = 11.25 cm

R – 112.5 kN

You could also measure the angle of R which is 22.5°.

3) If two forces are pulling at 90° to each other with the horizontal forces being 60 N and the vertical being 80 N, calculate the resultant.

96 forces | *What happens if forces act at an angle to each other?*

Answer:

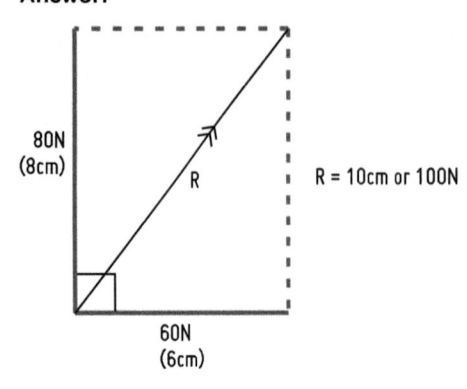

80N
(8cm)

60N
(6cm)

R = 10cm or 100N

Note it is a 90° angle so we just complete the rectangle.

R = 10 cm

R = 100 N

4) Find the resultant force 'R' if a force of 60 N acts in the vertical and 80 N is the horizontal plant, at an angle of 70° to each other.

Answer:

Again use the scale 1 cm = 10 N, so you should have drawn a parallelogram of 6 cm and 8 cm like the one below.

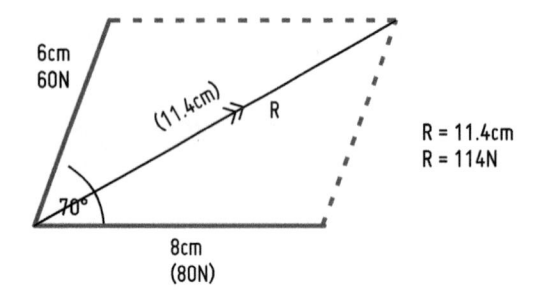

6cm
60N

(11.4cm) R

70°

8cm
(80N)

R = 11.4cm
R = 114N

Check on graph paper

R – 11.4 cm

R = 114 N

Resolving forces in two components (vertical and horizontal)

Sometimes we need to resolve vectors in both the vertical and horizontal directions. (This means we find out the vertical force and horizontal force.) Each vector is called a component.

Note: The general way to resolve forces vertically and horizontally is found using:

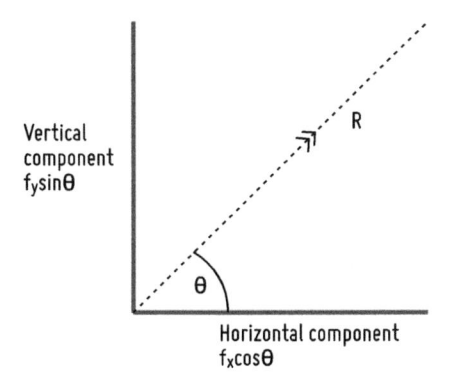

Vertical component
$f_y \sin\theta$

R

θ

Horizontal component
$f_x \cos\theta$

1) A pendulum pulls with a force of 300 N at an angle of 50°, as in the diagram below. Calculate the vertical and horizontal components acting on the pendulum.

   Note the angle is measured from the vertical.

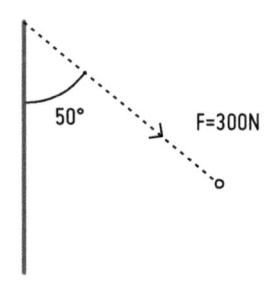

   50°   F=300N

   Vertical component:

   $Fy \, Sin \, \theta$

   $= Sin \, 50 \, \dfrac{Fy}{300N}$

   $Fy = Sin \, 50 \, \times \, 300$

   Fy = 230 Newtons

Horizontal component:

Fx Cos θ

$= \text{Cos } 50 \, \dfrac{Fx}{300N}$

$Fx = \text{Cos } 50 \times 300$

Fx = 193 Newtons

2) A dog is pulling on its lead at an angle of 45° with a force of 75 N. Calculate the horizontal and vertical components of this force.

Answer:
Vertical component:

Fy Sin θ

$= \text{Sin } 45° \, \dfrac{Fy}{75}$

$Fy = \text{Sin } 45 \times 75$

Fy = 53 Newtons

Horizontal component:

$Fx = \text{Cos } θ$

$= \text{Cos } 45 \, \dfrac{Fx}{75}$

$Fx = \text{Cos } 45 \times 75$

Fx = 53 Newtons

3) A man pulls a sledge with a cord over snow at an angle of 25° to the horizontal. The force he uses is 80 N. Calculate the vertical and horizontal components of this force.

Answer:
Vertically:

Fy Sin θ

$Fy = \text{Sin } 25 \times 80$

Fy = 34 Newtons

Horizontally:

Fx Cos θ

$Fx = \text{Cos } 25 \times 80$

Fx = 72.5 Newtons

Newton's laws of motion

Newton's first law of motion

"A mass will stay at rest or continue to move at a constant speed in a straight line unless a resultant force acts upon it."

This simply means objects will not move unless you push or pull them!

Secondly, if an object is moving it will carry on doing so in a straight line unless something pushes or pulls it to make a change in direction.

Newton's second law of motion

The acceleration of an object is directly proportional to the force applied producing that acceleration.

e.g. acceleration α force

"This means the harder you push an object, the quicker it will move."

Newton's third law of motion

To every action there is an equal and opposite reaction.

Note: forces always come in pairs

This is best explained by the example:

When you sit on a chair your weight (force) pushes down and the chair pushes back upwards an equal and opposite amount, stopping you sinking through the chair.

Moments and turning forces

(levers and seesaws)

A force which causes an object to turn is called a 'moment'.

The size of a moment is affected by the size of the force, position of the force and direction of the force.

The point at which an object turns around is called the 'pivot' or 'fulcrum'. We use moments all of the time in simple machines, see examples below:

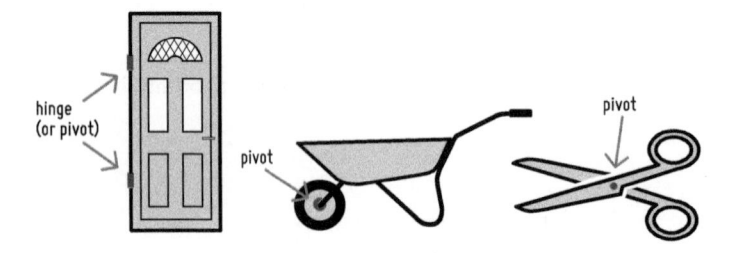

Simple machines make jobs easier: the first recorded simple machine was the lever. We find that the longer the handle of a lever, the easier it is to do a job. This is because the force is increased, and machines which do this are called 'force magnifiers'.

Moments are calculated using the formula:

Moment = force × perpendicular distance from the pivot

$M = f \times d$

Unit is the newton metre or Nm

1) Look at the two diagrams of a spanner below. Calculate the moment for each spanner and explain which spanner A or B would make turning the nut easier.

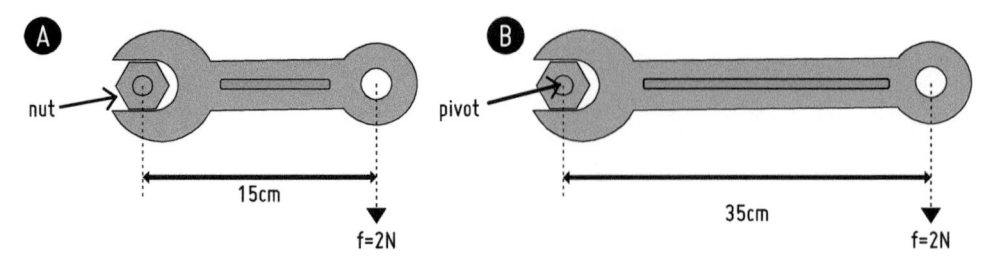

Moment produced by A:

$M = f \times d$

$= 2\,N \times 0.15\,m$

$M = \mathbf{0.3\,Nm}$

Moment produced by B:

M = f × d

= 2 N × 0.35 m

M = 0.70 Nm

Spanner B has a larger moment because the perpendicular distance from the pivot is greater, even though the force applied is the same in each case. This makes turning the nut easier and is an example of a force magnifier.

2) For each seesaw diagram below, calculate the moment on the left-hand side (LHS) and righthand side (RHS). Then say if the seesaw tips to the left, right, or remains horizontal in equilibrium.

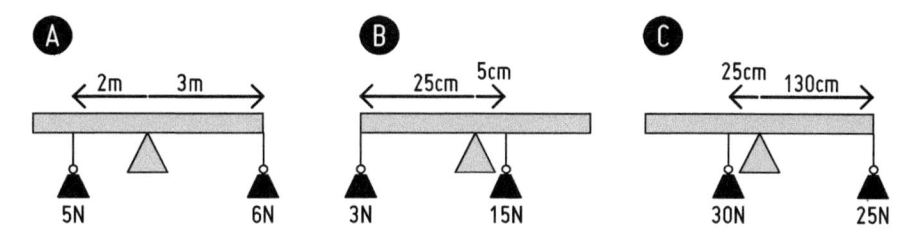

a)

A
2m, 3m
5N, 6N

B
25cm, 5cm
3N, 15N

C
25cm, 130cm
30N, 25N

Answer:

	LHS	RHS	Result
A	M = f × d = 2 × 5 M = 10 Nm	M = f × d = 6 × 3 M = 18 Nm	Tips to *right*
B	M = f × d = 3 × 0.25 M = 0.75 Nm	M = f × d = 15 × 0.05 M = 0.75 Nm	Balanced in *equilibrium*
C	M = f × d = 30 × 0.25 M = 7.5 Nm	M = f × d = 25 × 1.3 M = 32.5 Nm	Tips to *right*

Points to consider: Notice I changed the cm into metres and look at how I set out the calculations into LHS and RHS.

3) A crane has a counterweight of 93 kN which is suspended 15 m from the pivot. On the other side of the pivot is a load being lifted 40 m from the pivot. Calculate the size of the load using the following diagram for help.

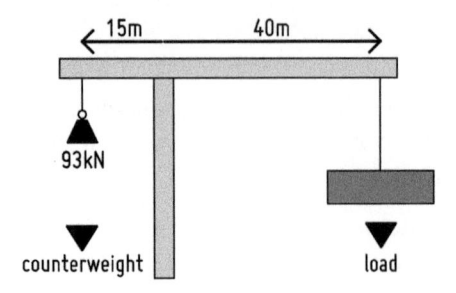

Answer:
First note the counterweight is 93 kN, meaning 93,000 N.

(LHS)

M = f × d

93,000 × 15

M = **1,395,000 Nm**

(RHS)

M = f × d

= f × 40

therefore 1,395,000 = f × 40 (if LHS = RHS)

$f = \dfrac{1,395,000}{40}$

f = 34,875 N or **35 kN**

4) Look at the diagram below of a crowbar lifting a heavy crate of goods. Calculate the force needed to lift the crate.

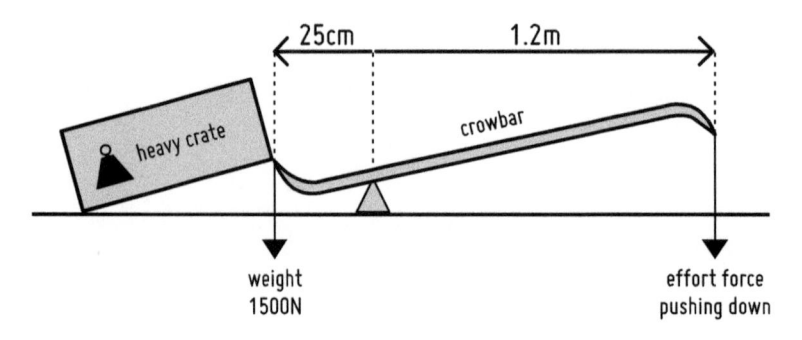

Answer:

Note: First of all, change the length 25 cm into metres (0.25 m) so the units are the same.

(LHS)

M = f × d

= 1500 × 0.25

M = 375 Nm

(RHS)

M = f × d

= f × 1.2

= 375 = f × 1.2

$f = \frac{375}{1.2}$

f = 312.5 N

Notice that 312.5 N can lift 1500 N using this simple machine: "the lever"!

5) A man is fishing in a river. He catches a fish, producing tension in the fishing line. The man pulls with a force of 80 N. He is holding the fishing rod 0.4 m from his end, the rod is 3 m in length.

Calculate:
a) the moment produced by the man pulling
b) the tension in the fishing line. (Note: The whole length of the rod should be considered.)

Answer:
Note: Draw a force diagram first to make it clear what is happening.

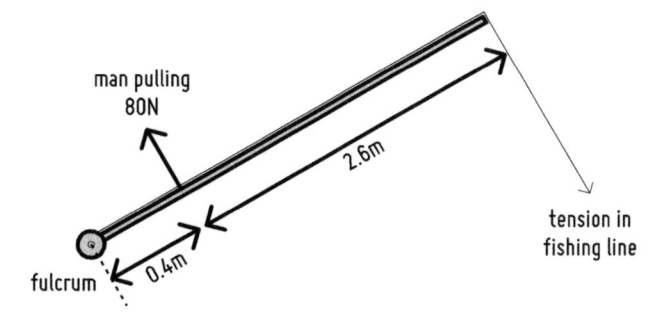

a) Moment produced by man pulling = f × d

   = 80 × 0.4

   = **32 Nm**

b) Tension in fishing line:

   LHS moment = RHS moment

   32 Nm = (0.4 + 2.6) × Tension

   32 Nm = 3 × T

   T = $\frac{32}{3}$ **10.6 N**

Gears

Gears are examples of simple machines which can make lifting heavy objects easier or make cars, motorbikes, trains or bicycles move faster using less effort. Gears will lose a lot of energy through friction producing heat, so they need to be lubricated to make them more efficient. Gears are circular wheels which rotate around an axel and are effectively a rotating lever. An example of this 'wheel and axel' principle is a car steering wheel, gear box, or gears and pedals on a bicycle. Gears can increase the force or turning effect so are often called force multipliers.

A cog wheel

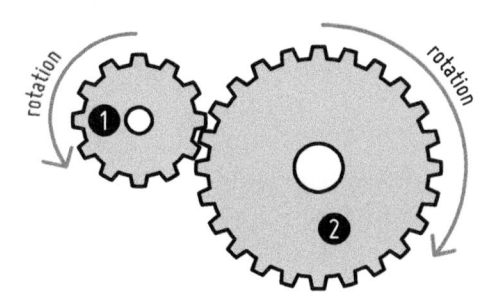

If we ignore the effects of friction in this section, as it would make the maths more difficult, we assume energy is conserved.

So energy transferred from cog 1 to cog 2 is:

force × distance moved by cog 1 = force × distance moved by cog 2

Cog 1 will turn further than cog 2 because it is smaller. The force exerted by cog 2 is therefore much greater. The second cog will also turn more slowly. This is what we might call 1st gear in a car. It is used to get the car moving from rest.

1) A small cog is used to turn a larger cog in a gear system. If the small cog has 20 teeth and the larger cog has 60 teeth, calculate the force produced on the large cog if 100 N is applied to the small cog.

   Answer:
   First calculate the magnifying effect using the formula:

   $$velocity\ ratio = \frac{number\ of\ teeth\ driven\ cog}{number\ of\ teeth\ on\ driver\ cog} = \frac{60}{20} = 3$$

   So the force is multiplied by 3 so the force produced by the larger cog is:

   3 × 100 = **300 N**

2) Top tour cyclists have used non-circular gears to improve their performance. Non-circular gears are thought to increase power produced by the rider. Use the diagram below to explain this theory:

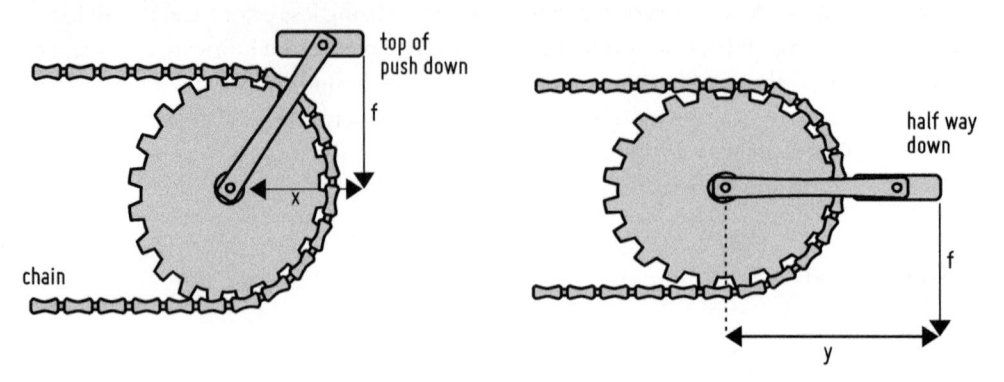

Answer:
The distance x increases to y halfway down the pedal revolution. The force is therefore increased as the pedal gets lower as the distance increases because the moment is calculated by force × distance from the pivot. This is an example of a force magnifier.

3) Two gear wheels are in contact. The first wheel has a radius of 60 mm and the second has a radius of 15 mm. Calculate the moment on each wheel if the first larger wheel has a force of 200 N applied to it.

Answer:
The 60 mm wheel:

moment = force × distance

= 200 N × 0.06 m (convert to metres)

= 12 N

The 15 mm wheel:

moment = force × distance

= 200 N × 0.015 m

= 3 N

Centre of mass (gravity)

This is the point at which all of the weight of an object appears to act. The downward force is produced by all the gravitational forces from each particle in an object acting as one. This point will affect how and where an object will balance.

A suspended mass will always come to rest with its centre of gravity exactly below where it is being suspended from.

1) Using a 'cone' as an example, explain 'stability' in terms of stable, unstable and neutral.

   Answer: (split the answer into three)
   a) Stable or in equilibrium

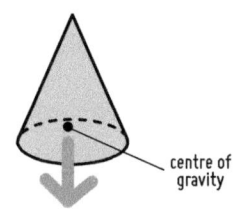

   In this position the cone is stable. The centre of gravity is at its lowest point over the base. It is said to be in equilibrium.

   b) Unstable

   The cone is upside down on its point. It is unstable. The centre of gravity is high above the base which is the tiny point. The centre of gravity can easily be moved over or away from the centre of the base, so the cone will easily fall.

   c) Neutral

   The centre of gravity remains in a constant position over the base. It does not rise or fall if the cone is pushed or acted upon by a force. It will simply roll about and come to rest in the same position. This is called 'neutral'.

Short revision questions on forces

1) Explain the following terms:
   a) displacement
   b) vector
   c) scalar
   d) magnitude

2) For the following diagram of a lever, label the effort, load and fulcrum (pivot).

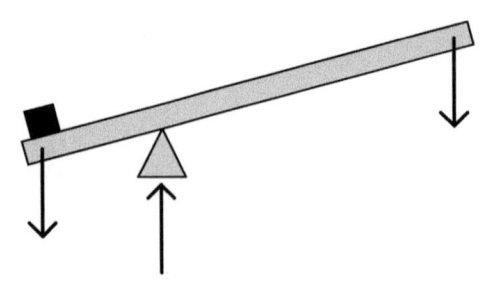

3) What should the force be on × to make the beam balance?

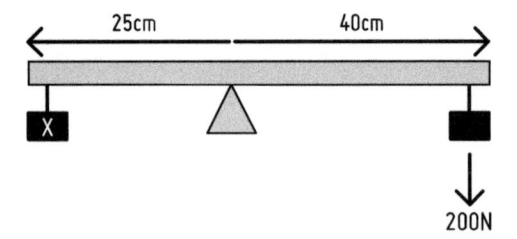

4) A driver cog has 8 teeth and drives a larger cog of 16 teeth. How much is the force magnified by?

5) A gear wheel has a radius of 30 mm and is turned by a force of 50 N. What is the moment produced on the wheel?

6) Define what we mean by 'centre of gravity'.

7) Two forces are acting at 60° to each other. The force in the horizontal plane is 6 N and in the vertical plane is 8 N. Calculate the resultant force using a parallelogram of forces scale diagram.

8) A pendulum pulls with a force of 200 N at an angle of 40°. Calculate the horizontal and vertical components of this action.

Answer:
1) a) Displacement is the distance between two places in a straight line.
   b) A vector is something which has magnitude and direction.
   c) A scalar has size or magnitude only.
   d) Magnitude is the size of something.
2) See question 4 in the worked examples.
3) 320 N.
4) 2.
5) 1.5 Nm.
6) The point at which the weight appears to act.
7) 12 N.
8) Horizontal = 153.6 N. Vertical = 128.6 N.

Motion graphs

When looking at motion graphs it is always very important to look at the axis first. This is because the graphs look very similar but mean very different things.

Note: Time is always on the bottom or horizontal axis.

Look at the examples below:

Distance time graphs

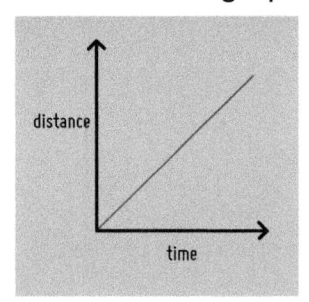

This shows a *constant or steady speed*. Notice the line increases by the same amount as time goes by; in other words, the object is moving from an observer, for example, by the same amount every second.

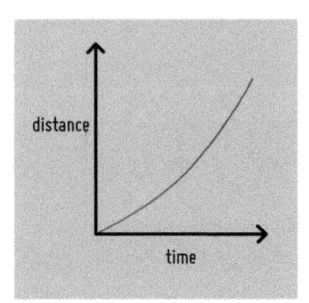

This shows an *acceleration*. This is because the line is a curve showing the distance is increasing with time at a different increasing rate, e.g. per second.

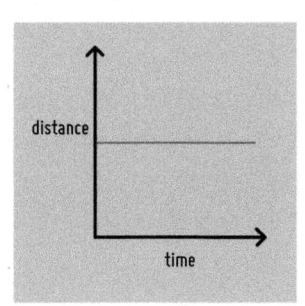

This shows an object *not moving*. The line does not move up or down on the vertical axis, time is just 'ticking by'.

Now, if we look at velocity (speed) time graphs you will see what I mean by checking the axis as the graphs look the same but mean very different things.

Velocity time graphs

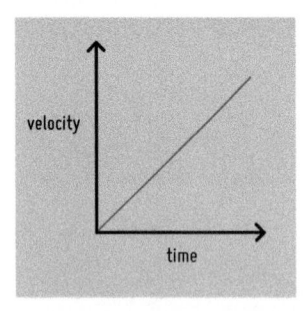

This shows an *acceleration* again but note it is a straight line, not a curve as you saw before. The velocity is increasing with time; it is not constant.

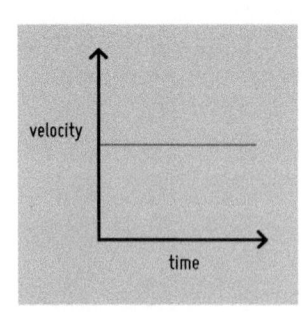

Note this looks like the stationary graph you saw before but actually it shows a *constant speed or velocity*. The line does not move up or down on the vertical axis, time ticks by, and the object keeps moving at a steady speed/velocity.

1) Use the following graph to describe the motion of a train during points A, B and C.

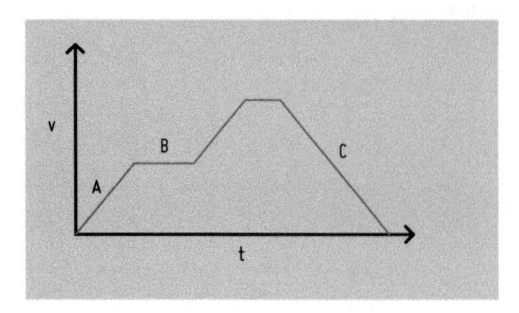

Answer:

A = Acceleration from rest

B = Constant velocity

C = Slowing down to rest

Note: Slowing down may be called deceleration or retardation.

2) Describe the motion of a car in the following graph at A, B and C.

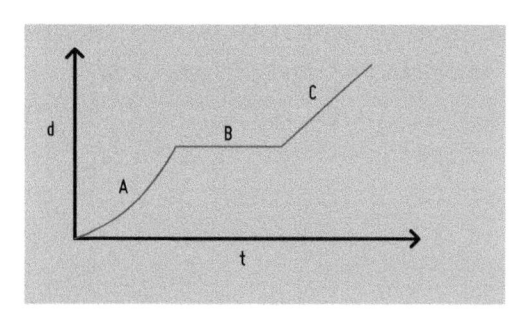

Answer:

a = accelerating

b = stopped

c = constant speed

3) A man is jogging at 3 m/s for 10 minutes: how far did he jog?

Answer:

First convert the minutes to seconds:

10 minutes = 10 × 60 = 600 seconds

Then rearrange the equation:

$$Speed = \frac{distance}{time} \rightarrow distance = speed \times time$$

Giving:

d = s × t

= 3 × 600

= **1800 m**

4) How fast is a car travelling if it covers 90 m in 3 seconds?

Answer:
Rearrange: $speed = \dfrac{distance}{time}$

To: $time = \dfrac{distance}{speed}$

$= \dfrac{90}{3}$

$= \mathbf{30\ m/s}$

5) How long does it take a cyclist to travel 3 km if the cyclist is moving at 12 m/s?

Answer:
First convert 3 km into metres = 3000 m

Next rearrange: $speed = \dfrac{distance}{time}$

To: $time = \dfrac{distance}{speed}$

$= \dfrac{3000}{12}$

= 250 seconds or **4 minutes 10 seconds**

6) A fast jet travels at 1400 km/h. How fast is it travelling per second?

Answer:
First calculate the speed in minutes from hours:

1400 km/h ÷ 60 = 23.3 km/min

Then to seconds:

23.3 km/min ÷ 60 = 0.38 km/second

Lastly convert the answer to m/s by multiplying 0.38 by 1000 as there are 1000 metres in one kilometre:

0.38 × 1000 = **380 m/s**

Acceleration

Acceleration is defined as "*the rate of change in velocity*". It is a *vector* quantity because velocity is a vector.

The formula to calculate acceleration is:

$$\text{Acceleration} = \frac{\text{final velocity} - \text{initial velocity}}{\text{time taken}}$$

Or:

$$a = \frac{v - u}{t}$$

The unit is m/s² which means metres per second per second.

1) A car is moving at 20 m/s and accelerates to 25/s in 5 seconds. Calculate its acceleration.

    Answer:
    $$a = \frac{v - u}{t}$$
    $$= \frac{25 - 20}{5}$$
    $$= \frac{5}{5}$$
    $$= 1 \text{ m/s}^2$$

2) How long does it take a lorry to accelerate from 4 m/s to 30 m/s if it accelerates at 5 m/s²?

    Answer:
    $$a = \frac{v - u}{t}$$
    $$= \frac{30 - 4}{t}$$
    $$5 = \frac{26}{t}$$
    $$t = \frac{26}{5}$$
    $$= 5.2 \text{ seconds}$$

3) A motorbike is travelling at 150 km/h. If it suddenly stops in 4 seconds, calculate its deceleration.

Answer:

First calculate the 150 km/h in m/s.

Per minute: 150 ÷ 60 = 2.5 km/m

Per second: 2.5 ÷ 60 = 0.0416 km/s

Them multiply by 1000 to put into m/s:

0.0416 × 1000 = 41.6 m/s

Now use:

$$a = \frac{v - u}{t}$$

$$= \frac{0 - 41.6}{4}$$

$$= -10.41 \text{ m/s}$$

Note: the answer is a negative number, showing it is slowing down.

4) Using the velocity time graph below, calculate the acceleration in the first 10 seconds and the total distance travelled in 40 seconds.

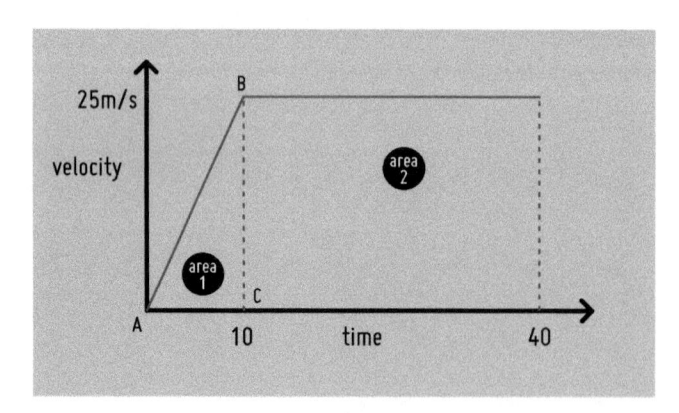

Note: Use the scales for distances up and across

Answer:

Acceleration for the first 10 seconds:

Acceleration is calculated by finding the 'slope' or 'gradient' of a line. This is calculated by dividing the distance 'up' by the distance 'across'. In this example the gradient in the first 10 seconds is:

$$\frac{B-C}{C-A} = \frac{25-0}{10-0} = 2.5 m/s^2$$

The total distance travelled is equal to the total area under the graph.

This is achieved by calculating the area of the triangle 1 added to area of rectangle 2.

Area of triangle 1:

½ b × h (base × height)

= ½ × 10 × 25

= 125 m

Area of rectangle 2:

b × h

= (40-10) × 25 (use the scale)

= 30 × 25

= 750 m

Total distance travelled:

= 125 + 750

= **875 m**

5) Calculate the acceleration over the first 30 seconds and total distance travelled for the graph below:

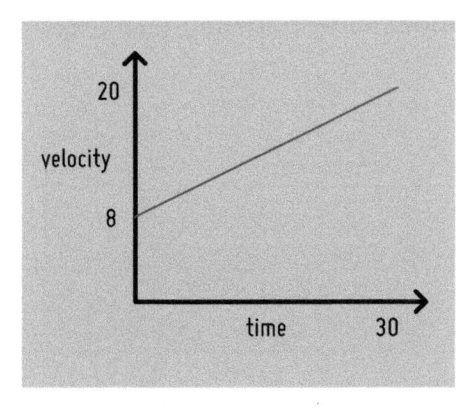

Answer:
First draw the area under the graph, making a triangle and a rectangle.

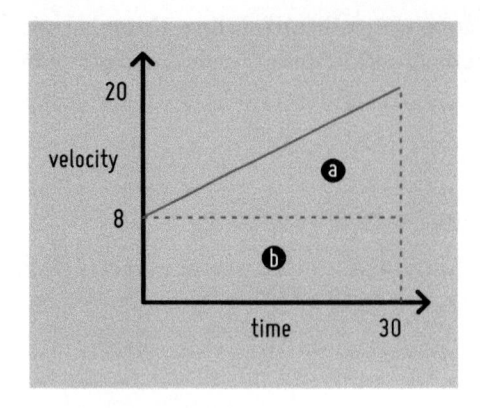

Acceleration = $\dfrac{v - u}{t}$

= $\dfrac{20 - 8}{30}$

= $\dfrac{12}{30}$

= $0.4 \, m/s^2$

Distance travelled:

Area of a:

½ b × h

= ½ × 30 × 12

= 180 m

Area of b:

b × h

= 30 × 8

= 240 m

Total distance travelled:

180 + 240

= **420 m**

6) For the following graph, calculate the acceleration in the first 10 seconds, acceleration between 40–70 seconds, and the total distance travelled.

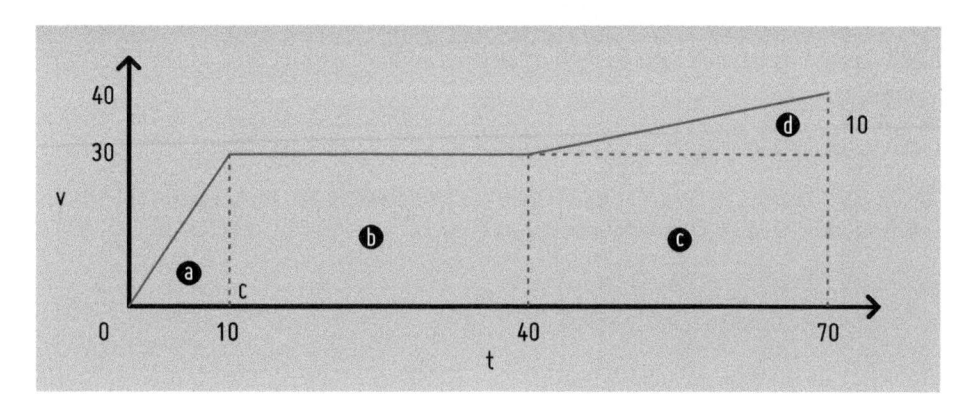

Answer:
Acceleration in the first 10 seconds:

$$\frac{v - u}{t}$$

$$= \frac{30 - 0}{10}$$

$$= \frac{30}{10}$$

$$= 3 \; m/s^2$$

Acceleration between 40-70 seconds:

$$\frac{v - u}{t}$$

$$= \frac{40 - 30}{30}$$

$$= \frac{10}{30}$$

$$= 0.33 \; m/s^2$$

Total distance travelled:

Add up areas A + B + C + D:

A = 1/2bh = ½ × 10 × 30 = 150

B = b × h = 30 × 30 = 900

C = b × h = 30 × 30 = 900

D = 1/2bh = ½ × 30 × 10 = 150

Total distance = **2100 m**

Newton's second law and its relationship between force, mass and acceleration

As already stated, the acceleration of an object is directly proportional to the force applied on that object.

Giving: *acceleration α force* (α = 'proportional to')

This means we have a graph like the one below; if we double the force we double the acceleration, or if we halve one we halve the other.

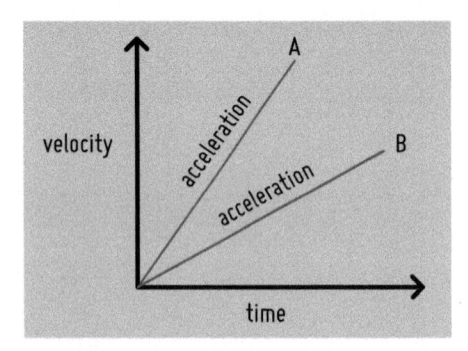

[Graph showing velocity vs time with two lines labelled A (steeper, "acceleration") and B (less steep, "acceleration")]

If the force on A is halved, the acceleration of B is halved. This means: force and acceleration are *directly proportional*.

Also: The second law can be considered in terms of momentum. "The rate of change of momentum of an object is proportional to the force applied in the direction of that force".

Giving: rate of change of momentum = $\frac{mv - mu}{t}$ which is proportional to the force, so:

$f \alpha \frac{mv - mu}{t}$

Factorising gives $f \alpha \, m \frac{v - u}{t}$ (note $\frac{v - u}{t}$ is acceleration)

So $f \alpha \, ma$

OR $f = ma$

This can be put into a triangular relationship:

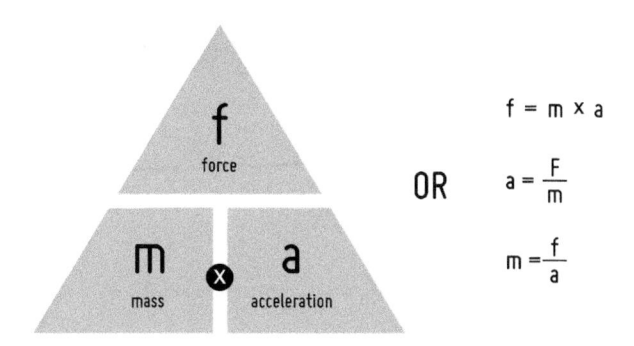

$$f = m \times a$$

OR

$$a = \frac{F}{m}$$

$$m = \frac{f}{a}$$

f = force

a = acceleration

m = mass

1) A car of 1300 kg mass produces a force of 3250 N of forward thrust. Calculate the acceleration produced.

   Answer:
   $$a = \frac{f}{m}$$
   $$= \frac{3250}{1300}$$
   $$= 2.5 \text{ m/s}^2$$

2) What force acts on an object if it has a mass of 12 kg and accelerates at 3 m/s²?

   Answer:
   $$f = m \times a$$
   $$f = 12 \times 3$$
   $$= 36 \text{ N}$$

3) If a bicycle accelerates at 9 m/s² and a force of 135 N is required to produce this acceleration, what is the mass of the bicycle? (ignore the rider)

   Answer:
   $$m = \frac{f}{a}$$
   $$m = \frac{135}{9}$$
   $$m = 15 \text{ kg}$$

4) Calculate the acceleration of a tractor of mass 450 kg if its engine produces 900 N of force.

Answer:

$a = \dfrac{f}{m}$

$a = \dfrac{900}{450}$

$a = 2 \text{ m/s}^2$

5) If a cyclist has a mass of 87 kg and accelerates at 3.5 m/s², what force is needed to produce this acceleration?

Answer:

f = m × a

f = 87 × 3.5

f = 304.5 N

6) A car has a mass of 1500 kg. If the car is travelling at 4 m/s and then increases to 12 m/s, calculate the acceleration of the car if the increase in speed took 2 seconds. Then calculate the force needed by the engine to produce this speed.

Answer:
The acceleration:

$a = \dfrac{v - u}{t}$

$= \dfrac{12 - 4}{2}$

$= \dfrac{8}{2}$

$= 4 \text{ m/s}^2$

The force required:

f = m × a

= 1500 × 4

= 6000 N

7) A car of mass 1600 kg has a forward force of 3000 N produced by the engine. A combined force of 700 N pushes against the car through air resistance and friction with the road. Calculate:

   i. the resultant forward force
   ii. acceleration of the car

Answer:
   i. Resultant force:

   $3000 - 7000$

   $= 2300 \text{ N}$

   ii. Acceleration of the car:

   $f = ma$

   $a = \dfrac{f}{m}$

   $a = \dfrac{2300}{600}$

   $= 3.83 \text{ m/s}^2$

8) A motorcycle crashes into a tree. The rider has a mass of 75 kg and decelerates to a complete stop in 1.2 seconds, after travelling at 15 m/s initially. Calculate:

   i. the deceleration of the rider
   ii. the force on the rider

Answer:
   i. $a = \dfrac{v - u}{t}$

   $= \dfrac{0 - 15}{1.2}$

   $= 12.5 \text{ m/s}$

   ii. $f = ma$

   $f = 75 \times -12.5$

   $f = -937.5 \text{ N}$

   OR – force acting on the rider is **937.5 N**

Short revision questions on motion graphs, acceleration and Newton's second law calculations

1) Look at the graph below and say what is happening at points A, B and C.

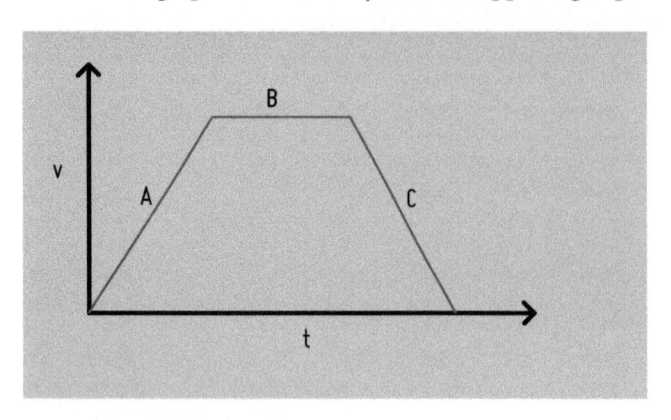

2) Study the graph below and the answer the following:
   i. What is the highest velocity reached?
   ii. How long does it take to reach the highest speed?
   iii. What is the acceleration in the first 10 seconds?
   iv. How far did the object travel?

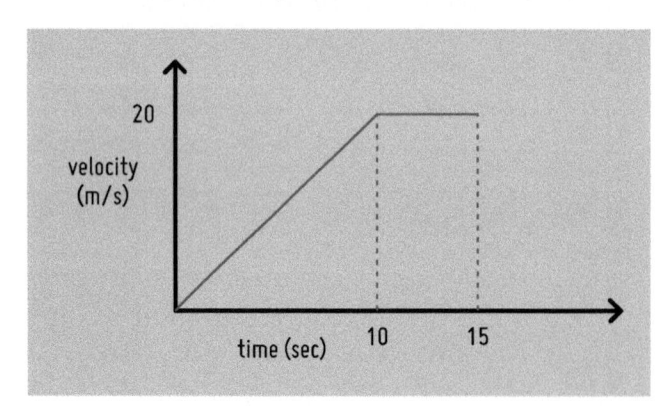

3) A bullet is fired from a gun and reaches a speed of 400 m/s in 0.20 seconds. Calculate the acceleration of the bullet.

4) In 2009 Usain Bolt ran 100 m in 9.58 seconds. Calculate the overall acceleration he achieved.

   (Calculate average speed first.)

5) A sports car manufacturer claims its car can accelerate from 0-60 mph in 5 seconds.

   Calculate the overall acceleration of this car. (Note 60 mph = 26.82 m/s.)

6) Calculate the mass of an object if it has an acceleration of 5 m/s² and is acted upon by a force of 25 N.

7) Calculate the force on a 320 kg object which makes it accelerate at 2 m/s².

8) Calculate the force produced to make a 220 kg motorbike accelerate at 3 m/s².

9) Calculate the change in acceleration of an object of mass 3 kg which is acted upon by a force of 25 N which increases to 37 N. (Hint: calculate the increase in force then the acceleration.)

10) A girl on a skateboard accelerates at 2.2 m/s on a halfpipe with a force of 110 N. Calculate the girl's weight in Newtons. (Hint: check the relationship between mass and weight) (g = 10 N/kg)

126 WORKSPACE FOR SELF-TESTING

WORKSPACE FOR SELF-TESTING

Answers
1) A: acceleration. B: constant velocity. C: deceleration.
2)
   i. 20 m/s
   ii. 10 seconds
   iii. 2 m/s^2
   iv. 200 m
3) 2000 m/s^2
4) 1.09 m/s^2
5) 5.364 m/s^2
6) 5 kg
7) 640 N
8) 660 N
9) 4 m/s^2
10) 500 N

Momentum

Momentum is a product of mass and velocity. This can be represented by the equation:

momentum = mass × velocity

Note: use kg when calculating momentum

Momentum has the units kg.m/s, since it is calculated by multiplying mass and velocity. It can be placed in a formula triangle as below:

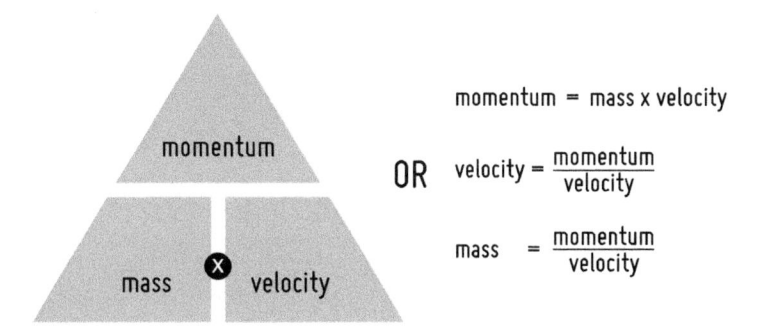

OR

momentum = mass × velocity

velocity = $\frac{momentum}{velocity}$

mass = $\frac{momentum}{velocity}$

Heavy objects need more force to get them moving and larger forces to stop them once they are moving.

Note: If two objects are of different masses and are acted upon by equal forces, the lighter of the two will gain higher velocity compared to the heavier object, but they will have the same momentum.

1) A toy train of mass 0.6 kg is rolling down a slope at 70 cm/s. Calculate its momentum.

   Answer:
   First convert the cm/s into m/s:

   70 cm/s = 0.7 m/s

   Then use the formula:

   momentum = mass × velocity

   = 0.6 × 0.7

   = **0.42 kg.m/s**

2) Calculate the momentum of a cyclist whose combined mass is 115 kg (person and bicycle), who is moving at 12 m/s.

Answer:
momentum = mass × velocity

= 115 × 12

= **1380 kg.m/s**

3) Calculate the mass of a golf ball if it has a momentum of 2.5 kg.m/s and it is moving at 25.5 m/s.

Answer:
$$mass = \frac{momentum}{velocity}$$

$$= \frac{2.5}{25.5}$$

= **0.098 kg (98 g)**

4) A car of mass 1400 kg has a momentum of 42,000 kg.m/s. Calculate the car's velocity.

Answer:
$$velocity = \frac{momentum}{mass}$$

$$= \frac{42,000}{1400}$$

= **30 m/s**

Momentum and collisions

The momentum before a collision is equal to the momentum after a collision. This is called the conservation of momentum. This can be expressed mathematically:

$$m_1 \times v_1 = m_2 \times v_2$$

Where m_1 and m_2 are masses, and v_1 and v_2 are velocities.

To solve problems of this nature, divide the problem into two halves. See the way I have set the problem out below:

1) A trolley of 0.7 kg is moving at 1.4 m/s and collides and joins with a second trolley of mass 0.6 kg. Calculate the velocity of the two trolleys after the collision if they join together and move off.

Answer:

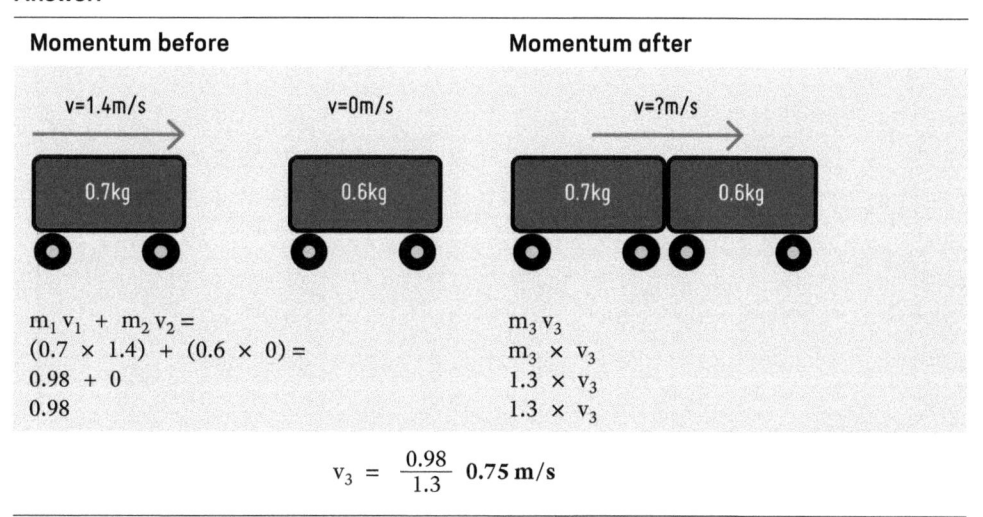

Momentum before	Momentum after
v=1.4m/s v=0m/s	v=?m/s
0.7kg 0.6kg	0.7kg 0.6kg
$m_1 v_1 + m_2 v_2 =$	$m_3 v_3$
$(0.7 \times 1.4) + (0.6 \times 0) =$	$m_3 \times v_3$
$0.98 + 0$	$1.3 \times v_3$
0.98	$1.3 \times v_3$

$$v_3 = \frac{0.98}{1.3} \quad 0.75 \text{ m/s}$$

Note: momentum before = momentum after

2) A railway truck full of coal is moving at 4 m/s and has a combined mass of 6000 kg. It collides with a stationary truck of mass 1000 kg. The trucks move off together. Calculate the velocity of the joined trucks after the collision.

Answer:

Momentum before	Momentum after
$m_1 v_1 + m_2 v_2 =$	$m_3 v_3$
$(6000 \times 4) + (1000 \times 0) =$	$7000 \times v_3$
$24{,}000 + 0$	$7000 \times v_3$

$$v_3 = \frac{24{,}000}{7000} \quad 3.42 \text{ m/s}$$

3) A pistol of mass 1.2 kg fires a bullet of 15 g at 420 m/s. Calculate the recoil of the gun when it fires the bullet.

Answer:
First put values into order.

m_1 = mass of gun. v_1 = recoil. m_2 = mass of bullet. v_2 = speed of bullet.

$m_1 \times v_1 = m_2 \times v_2$ if momentum is conserved, so:

$1.2 \times v_1 = 0.015 \times 420$

$1.2 \times v_1 = 6.3$

$V_1 = \frac{6.3}{1.2}$

$= 5.25$ m/s

Note: I converted the mass of bullet into kg from g

The force of impact during a collision

When an object has a collision of any sort the force produced depends upon: mass of object, change in velocity, and the time the collision lasts. In essence the quicker an object comes to rest the larger the impact force. This is summarised by the equation below:

$$force = \frac{mass \times velocity\ change}{time\ taken\ for\ collision}$$

Note: Car manufacturers try and make collisions last longer to reduce the impact force on the passengers using techniques like crumple zones.

1) A boy is running at 3.2 m/s and accidentally runs into a lamppost, coming to a stop in 2.4 seconds. The boy has a mass of 65 kg. Calculate the impact on the boy.

   Answer:
   $$f = \frac{m \times a}{t}$$
   $$= \frac{65 \times (0 - 3.2)}{2.4}$$
   $$= 86.6\ N$$

   Note: I used 'a' as change in velocity as the rate of change in velocity is acceleration, but in this case it is deceleration. Also the '0' is used as the boy has come to rest, i.e. stationary.

2) A bullet has a mass of 12 g. It is fired from a gun into a target. The bullet is travelling at 450 m/s just before it hits the target. The bullet embeds itself into the target and comes to rest in 1/100 of a second. Calculate the impact force produced by the bullet.

   Answer:
   $$f = \frac{m \times a}{t}$$
   $$= \frac{0.012 \times (0 - 450)}{0.01}$$
   $$= 540\ N$$

   Note: I converted the mass into kg and the time into seconds.

3) A satellite of mass 2000 kg fires its boosters for 7 seconds to adjust its orbit. The satellite is accelerated from rest to 20 m/s in this time. Calculate the force produced by the boosters.

Answer:

$$f = \frac{m \times a}{t}$$

$$= \frac{2000 \times (0 - 20)}{7}$$

$$= 5714.3 \text{ N}$$

> Note: In this example we can think of the force as being a change in momentum, e.g. $f = \frac{m \times v}{t}$ as mv = momentum

The 'pushing' force in this example would be called 'impulse'.

4) A 20 g dart is thrown at a dartboard and comes to rest in 0.05 seconds. If the dart was thrown at 3 m/s calculate:

   i. the impact force
   ii. momentum during flight
   iii. kinetic energy during flight

Answer:

i. $f = \frac{ma}{t}$

$$= \frac{0.02 \times (0 - 3)}{0.05}$$

$$= \frac{0.06}{0.05}$$

$$= 1.2 \text{ N}$$

ii. momentum = m × v

$$= 0.02 \times 3$$

$$= 0.06 \text{ kg.m/s}$$

iii. ke = ½ mv²

$$= ½ \times 0.02 \times 3^2$$

$$= ½ \times 0.02 \times 9$$

$$= 0.09 \text{ J}$$

5) Explain how the following car safety features help to protect passengers during a collision:

   i. crumple zones
   ii. seat belts
   iii. airbags

   Answer:
   i. Crumple zones. When a car crashes, the front and back are designed to 'fold or crumple'. A moving car has kinetic energy; this energy is transferred into deforming the 'crumple zone' beyond the material's elastic limit. The energy is dissipated. Also, the time for the collision is extended, which reduces the impact force.

   ii. Seat belts. During a collision, the passenger will move forward unless restrained, as the passenger is not part of the car and will have their own momentum. If the seat belt is not worn the passenger will collide with a hard surface (dashboard or windscreen) and stop suddenly, producing a large impact force. If the belt is worn they stretch slightly and hold the passenger in place. Because the belt stretches it reduces the force of impact as the time for collision is increased. Also the passengers should not collide with a hard surface.

   iii. Airbags. When a collision occurs the bag inflates. If this happens the passenger will move forward; their weight and forward force squash the bag, and it deflates slowly, reducing the impact force and increasing the collision time. The airbag is made as large as possible as a large surface area will decrease the pressure on the bag and therefore the impact force on the passenger.

Short revision questions on momentum and collisions

1) A cannon ball of mass 5 kg is fired out of a cannon at 150 m/s. Calculate the momentum of the cannon ball.

2) A footballer kicks a 0.5 kg football and produces a momentum of 12.5 kg.m/s. How fast was the ball moving?

3) A toy truck of mass 5 kg is moving at 3 m/s. It collides with another truck of mass 2 kg, which is stationary. The trucks join together and move off together after the collision. Calculate the velocity of the joined trucks after the collision.

4) Calculate the recoil velocity of a cannon if it has a mass of 1000 kg and the cannon ball fired has a mass of 15 kg and velocity of 30 m/s.

5) A car of mass 1700 kg crashes into a wall at 30 m/s and comes to rest on 0.10 seconds. Calculate the force of impact during this collision.

6) Explain why children's play areas have soft rubber floors. Refer to impact, forces and time for collision in your answer.

WORKSPACE FOR SELF-TESTING 137

Answers:
1) 750 kg.m/s.
2) 25 m/s.
3) 2.14 m/s.
4) 2.2 m/s.
5) 5.1×10^5 N
6) Answer should refer to increasing time of collision to reduce impact force.

Pressure

Pressure is defined as the force per unit area of an object. This generally means large surface areas produce small pressure, and small surface areas produce large pressure.

Pressure is a force so we measure it in Newtons (N) per metre squared, as it acts on an area.

Sometimes you may see the unit Pa (Pascal) which is one Newton of force acting on one metre squared. Pascal was a French mathematician and scientist whom the unit is named after.

The classic example of thinking about pressure and surface area is with the humble drawing pin. We push a drawing pin into a board using the large, round side because this produces much less pressure on your thumb than on the pointed side. The point has a very high pressure because of its small surface area, making it very sharp.

Calculating pressure we use the formula:

$$pressure = \frac{force}{area} \qquad p = \frac{F}{A}$$

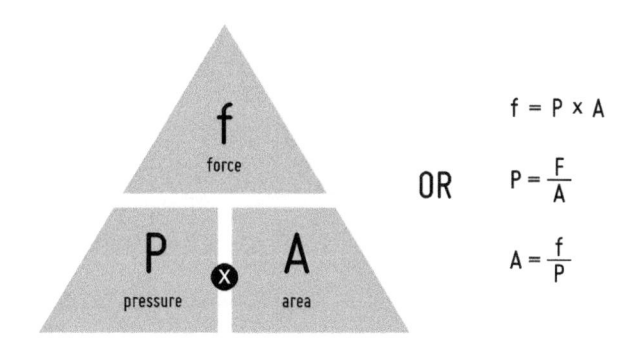

OR

$$f = P \times A$$
$$P = \frac{F}{A}$$
$$A = \frac{f}{P}$$

1) A toolbox has a surface area in contact with the ground of 0.7 m². The mass of the toolbox is 4 kg. Calculate the pressure produced by the box.

   Answer:
   First convert 4 kg into Newtons by multiplying by 10, giving 40 N.

   Then use: $pressure = \frac{force}{area}$

   $= \frac{40}{0.7}$

   $= 57.14 \text{ N/m}^2$

2) A girl has a mass of 65 kg and the total surface area of both feet in contact with the ground is 175 cm².

   i. calculate the pressure she produces with both feet on the ground.

   ii. assuming both feet are identical, show what would happen to the pressure if she stood on one leg.

   Answers:
   i. First convert 65 kg into Newtons = 650 N

   $$pressure = \frac{force}{area}$$

   $$= \frac{650}{175}$$

   $$= 3.71 \text{ N/cm}^2 \text{ (for both feet)}$$

   ii. If she stood on one foot the area is $\frac{175}{2}$ = 87.5 cm²

   $$p = \frac{F}{A}$$

   $$= \frac{650}{87.5}$$

   $$= 7.42 \text{ N/cm}^2$$

   Note: 7.42 is 2 × 3.71, so the pressure would be double on one foot!

   Note: the answers to this question are in cm². To convert to metres squared we need to remember that 1 m² is 10,000 cm² (100 × 100 = 10,000). So to convert to m² we need to multiply each answer by 10,000.

3) Calculate the pressure produced by the heel of a shoe in metres squared if the heel is 3 cm² and the person wearing the shoe has a weight of 700 N.

   Answer:
   3 ÷ 10,000 = 0.0003

   $$p = \frac{F}{A}$$

   $$= \frac{700}{0.0003}$$

   $$= 2.3 \times 10^6 \text{ N/m}^2$$

4) A book is placed on a table. What is the area of the contact surface if the book has a mass of 500 g and produces a pressure of 111.1 N/m²?

Answer:

$$A = \frac{F}{p}$$

$$= \frac{5}{111.1}$$

$$= 0.045 \text{ m}^2$$

Pressure in liquids

> **Note:**
> 1. pressure acts in every possible direction in a liquid
> 2. pressure is transmitted through liquids
> 3. pressure increases with depth

To calculate the pressure produced by a column of liquid we use the equation:

$p = h \times \rho \times g$

p = pressure

h = height of liquid column

ρ = density

g = gravitational field strength (N/kg)

> Note: ρ is the symbol for density: it is the Greek letter 'rho'.

1) Calculate the pressure produced by a column of air on the ground if the column is 2 km high and the density of the air is 1.3 kg/m³. Take 'g', the gravitational field strength, to be 9.8 N/kg.

    Answer:
    $p = h\rho g$

    $= 2000 \times 1.3 \times 9.8$

    $= 25480$ Pa OR $\mathbf{2.5 \times 10^4}$ **Pa**

2) Seawater density is greater than fresh water because it contains salt. If we take the density of seawater to be 1027 kg/m³, calculate the pressure at a depth of:

    i. 10 m

    ii. 20 m

    For this question $g = 9.8$ N/kg

    Answer:

    i. at 10 m:

    $p = h\rho g$

    $= 10 \times 1027 \times 9.8$

    $= 100646$

    $= \mathbf{1 \times 10^5}$ **Pa**

ii. at 20 m:

$p = h\rho g$

$= 20 \times 1027 \times 9.8$

$= 201292$

$= 2.01 \times 10^5$ Pa

3) A submarine dives into deep water and experiences a pressure of 5,032,300 Pa.

Calculate how deep the submarine has gone. Density of seawater is 1027 kg/m³ and g = 9.8 N/kg.

Answer:

$p = h\rho g$ so $h = \dfrac{p}{\rho \times g}$

$h = \dfrac{5032300}{1027 \times 9.8}$

$h = \dfrac{5032300}{10064.6}$

$= 500$ m

4) Look at the mercury barometer in the diagram below.

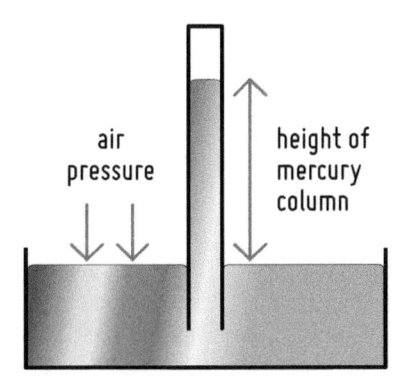

The height of the column of mercury is used to calculate air pressure. The average height of mercury at sea level is 760 mm. This changes with the weather, so a barometer is used to predict weather conditions. Using the following data; density of mercury = 13,600 kg/m³ and g = 10 N/kg, calculate the air pressure when the column is:

i. 760 mm
ii. 800 mm
iii. 700 m

iv. state a conclusion between column height and air pressure

Answer:

Use the formula $p = h\rho g$ for each case

i. $p = h\rho g$

      $= 0.76 \times 13{,}600 \times 10$

      $= 103{,}360$

      $= \mathbf{103{,}000 \text{ Pa}}$

Note: the mm is converted into m

ii. $p = h\rho g$

      $= 0.80 \times 13{,}600 \times 10$

      $= 108{,}800$

      $= \mathbf{109{,}000 \text{ Pa}}$

Note: I have rounded up the answer to make it clear.

iii. $p = h\rho g$

      $= 0.70 \times 13{,}600 \times 10$

      $= 95{,}200$

      $= \mathbf{95 \text{ kPa}}$

Note: I have rounded down the answer to make it clear.

iv. My conclusion is that as the atmospheric pressure increases, the column height increases.

Hint: kPa means kilo Pascals, e.g. $\times 1000$

Short revision questions on pressure

1) A suitcase has a mass of 8.5 kg. Calculate the pressure on the ground when it is:

   i. lying flat
   ii. upright

   The dimensions are as follows: 1.2 × 0.75 × 0.24 (metres) and take gravity (g) to be 10 N/kg.

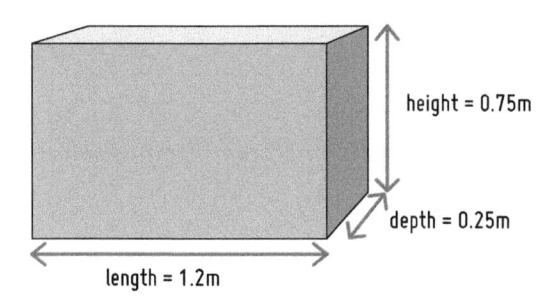

   height = 0.75m
   depth = 0.25m
   length = 1.2m

2) An object produces a pressure of 25 Pa on the ground. If its area is 3 m², what is the force produced by this object?

3) Calculate the pressure a pound coin produces if it is lying face down on a table. The mass of a pound coin is 0.00875 kg (8.75 g) and its diameter is 22.5 mm. Take g to be 10 N/kg and the area of a circle to be πr^2.

4) Explain why a tractor has wide wheels for working on a farm in terms of pressure.

5) A concrete column is used to support a building. If the column is 8 m high and the density of concrete is about 2400 kg/m³, taking g to be 10 N/kg, what is the pressure produced by this column on the ground?

6) A swimming pool is 3 m deep and is filled with fresh water of density 1000 kg/m³. Taking the gravitational field strength to be 9.8 N/kg, calculate the pressure at the bottom of the pool

146 WORKSPACE FOR SELF-TESTING

Answer:

1) i. 94.4 N/m^2

   ii. 453.33 N/m^2

2) 75 N

3) 0.022 kg/m^2

4) Wide wheels exert less pressure on the ground so they don't sink into soft ground or mud easily.

5) 192 kPa

6) 29.4 kPa

WAVES

Generally speaking, we can say there are two types of wave, which are mechanical and electromagnetic. Mechanical waves are things like ripples on a pool, and electromagnetic waves are things like radio waves.

We can further split up waves into two groups again: transverse and longitudinal waves. You will be expected to describe the properties, uses and examples of different types of waves.

You will also be expected to use the wave equation, which is seen below, to calculate speed, frequency and wavelength of waves.

The wave equation:

velocity = frequency × wavelength

$v = f \times \lambda$

> Note: λ is a Greek letter called lambda which we use for wavelength.

The units are:

velocity (v) = m/s

frequency (f) = Hz (hertz)

wavelength (λ) = m

> Key point: what is a wave?

Energy is transported from place to place by waves. The particles in a material (medium) vibrate and pass on the energy. The material, however, does not move itself from its position.

1) Describe transverse and longitudinal waves, giving examples of each.

   Answer:
   Transverse:
   The word 'transverse' means to cross something or 'made at right angles'. A transverse wave is one in which the movements of energy and vibration are at right angles to each other or 90° to each other. Consider the diagram below:

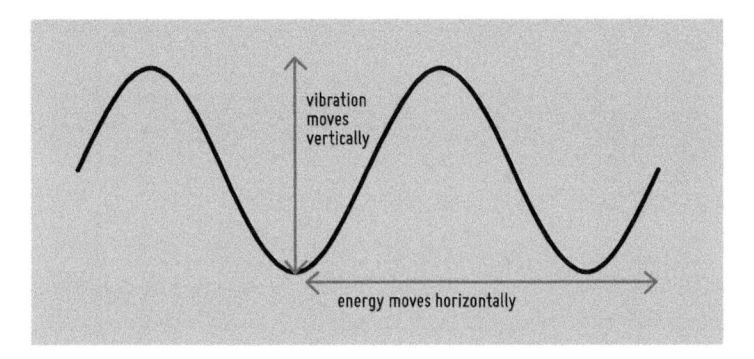

   Examples: light, ripples on a pond, all electromagnetic waves

   Longitudinal:
   These waves are sometimes called 'compression' waves as parts of the wave are squashed up. The energy and vibration are in the same plane, see below:

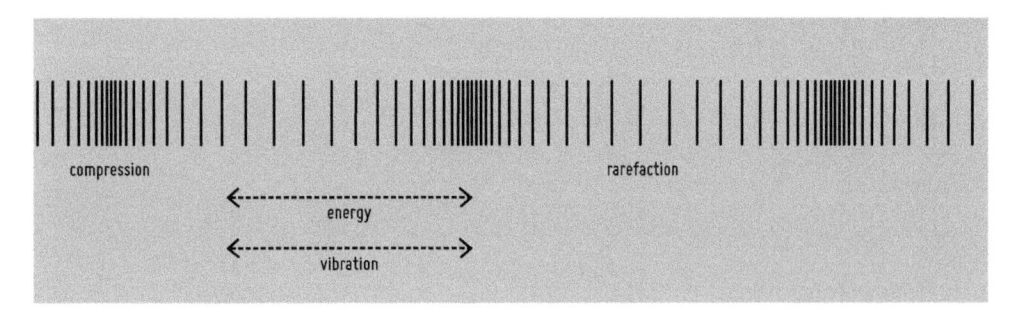

   Note the compression is where the molecules are 'squashed' together. A rarefaction is where the wave looks stretched and the molecules are far apart.

   Examples: sound, seismic waves, ultrasound

150 WAVES

2) Using the diagram below, describe what we mean by the following words: amplitude, wavelength, frequency and wave speed.

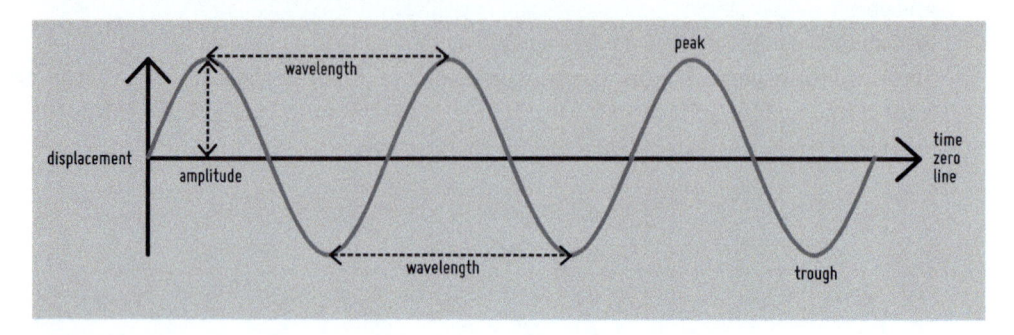

Answer:

Amplitude (A)
This is the 'maximum displacement from rest'. This means if the zero line is the start, amplitude is how high or low the wave gets from this point.

> **Note:** A common mistake students make is to label amplitude as the total height from a trough to a peak. See next diagram:

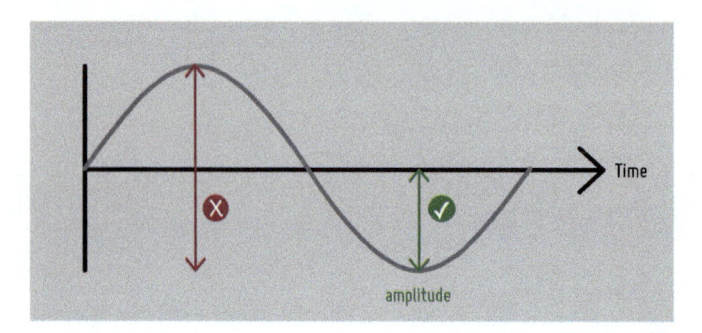

Wavelength (λ)
This is the distance between two identical points on a wave. Notice I have drawn two examples: one from peak to peak, and the other from trough to trough. You could choose a third, which starts at time zero and comes back up to the zero line. This third method, however, often confuses students.

> **Note:** I usually tell my students to learn one method of measuring λ and stick to that!

Frequency (f)

Frequency is the time it takes for one wavelength to pass a point per second. I tell students it is effectively the number of 'bumps' per second passing through a point! Frequency is measured in a unit called the hertz (Hz) after Heinrich Hertz who was a German physicist who confirmed the existence of electromagnetic waves. The unit is correctly defined as the number of wave cycles per second.

Consider the following diagrams:

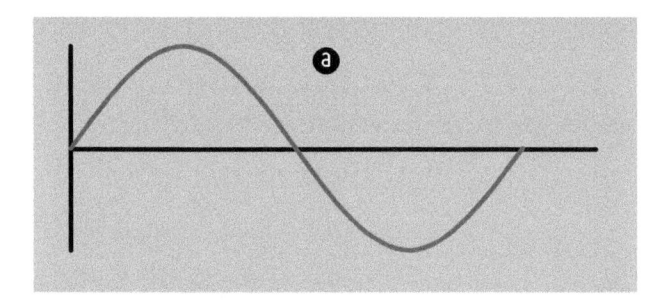

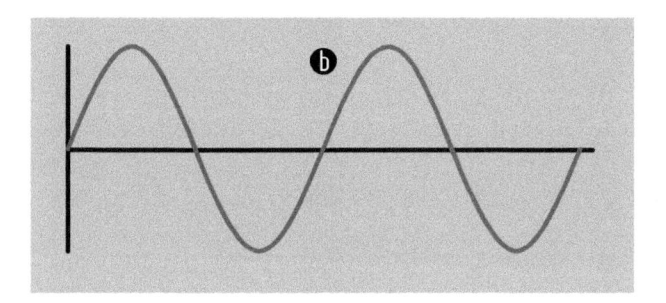

Diagram A has a long wavelength, whereas B has a short wavelength. This means that A has a low frequency, and B has a high frequency. Notice they are both the same height above and below the zero line, so they have the same amplitude.

Lastly, long wavelength, low frequency waves like radio waves, have low energy, whereas short wavelength, high-frequency waves like gamma waves, have high energy.

3) A wave has a wavelength of 20 m and a frequency of 500 Hz. Calculate the speed of the wave.

Answer:

$v = f \times \lambda$

$ = 500 \times 20$

$ = 10,000 \text{ m/s}$

4) A wave has a wavelength of 100 cm and has a speed of 3 × 10⁸ m/s. What is its frequency?

Answer:
Firstly, 100 cm = 1 m

$$f = \frac{v}{\lambda}$$

$$= \frac{3 \times 10^8}{1}$$

$$= 3 \times 10^8 \text{ Hz}$$

5) Calculate the wavelength of a wave if its frequency is 15 Hz and it is moving at 2000 m/s.

Answer:

$$\lambda = \frac{v}{f}$$

$$= \frac{2000}{15}$$

$$= 133.3 \text{ m/s}$$

Frequency can also be calculated using the formula:

$$frequency = \frac{1}{time\ period} \text{ OR } f = \frac{1}{T} \text{ (Note: time period = T)}$$

The time period is the time for a complete oscillation. A complete oscillation is a complete wave, complete swing of a pendulum, or a complete stretch and return to zero of a spring. It is the time between two identical points on a wave, like between two peaks or two troughs.

6) Calculate the frequency of the following waves with the following time periods:

   i. 0.25 seconds

   ii. 1.2 seconds

   iii. 3 seconds

Answer:

i. $f = \dfrac{1}{T}$

　　$= \dfrac{1}{0.25}$

　　$= 4 \text{ Hz}$

ii. $f = \dfrac{1}{T}$

　　$= \dfrac{1}{1.2}$

　　$= 0.83 \text{ Hz}$

iii. $f = \dfrac{1}{T}$

　　$= \dfrac{1}{3}$

　　$= 0.3 \text{ Hz}$

Reflection

Reflection is studied in the classroom by investigating light beams in mirrors or ripples of water in a ripple tank. We must always remember light travels in straight lines. We use specific words in this topic which you need to learn so you can understand the theory and what questions are asking. They are as follows:

Normal

This is an imaginary line drawn at 90º to the surface of a mirror, glass block or the interface between two mediums.

Medium

A material which a wave travels through.

Incident beam

Light leaving a light source and travelling towards an object.

Reflected beam

Light beam which reflects off something.

Angle of incidence

An angle measured from the normal to the incident beam.

Angle of reflection

Angle from the normal to reflected beam.

7) i. Describe what we mean by reflection of light in a 'plane' mirror, including the laws of reflection.

   ii. Draw a labelled diagram to illustrate reflection in a 'plane' mirror.

   Answer:
   i. The incident and reflected rays leave and enter the mirror at the same angle; or to put it another way: 'the angle of incidence = the angle of reflection'. This is the first law of reflection. The second law states that the incident, reflected beam and normal beam are all in the same plane, which means that they can be drawn on flat paper (it is not 3D).

ii.

i_i = angle of incidence
i_r = angle of reflection

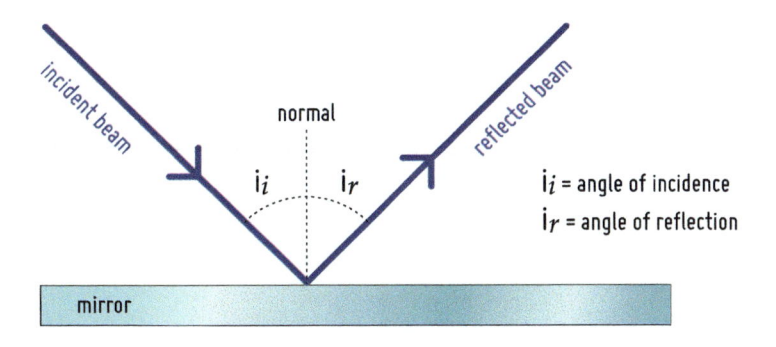

i^i = angle of incidence

ir = angle of reflection

Note: small angled lines show the back of mirror

8) What can you say about the image in a flat-plane mirror and draw a diagram to show how the image is formed.

Answer:
Firstly, this example concerns a normal mirror you may find in your house. It is a flatplane mirror so the image you see is the same size as the object (think about when you look in a normal mirror you are neither smaller or larger!). The second point is that the image is formed at the same distance behind the mirror as the image is in front of the mirror. Lastly, the image is 'laterally inverted' which means turned around (think of writing in a mirror – it is backwards).

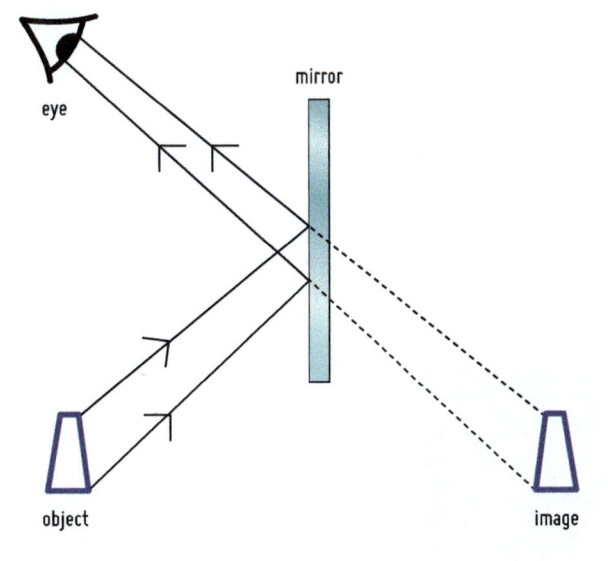

156 WAVES | *Reflection*

9) Describe, with the aid of a diagram, what we mean by refraction.

   Answer:
   Quite simply, refraction is the bending of light when a beam or ray of light passes from one medium to another. A common example is when a beam passes from air through glass and back out. How much the light bends depends upon the angle the beam enters the second medium, and the optical density of the medium. See the diagram below:

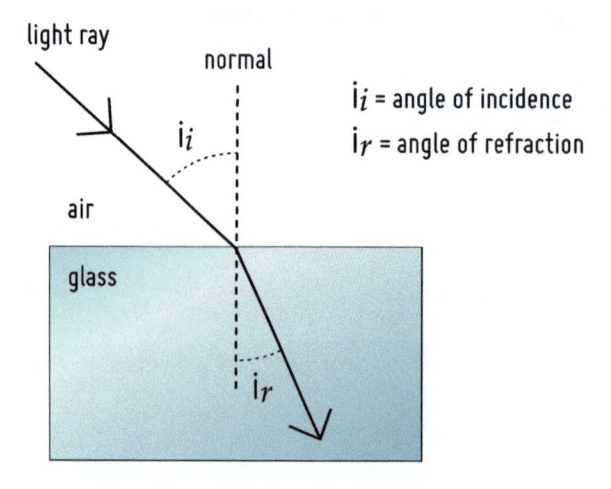

   i_i = angle of incidence
   i_r = angle of refraction

   i^i = angle of incidence

   i_r = angle of reflection

   Notice the light way bends towards the normal when it enters the glass block.

10) With the use of diagrams explain why light refracts when it enters a medium (material) of different optical density.

    Answer:
    The classic analogy to explain why light refracts is to think about a car on a road which encounters a strip of mud at an angle. See the diagram below:

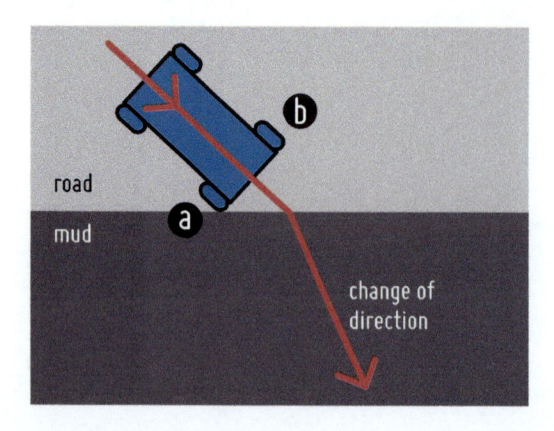

Answer:
The wheel at A reaches the mud before the wheel at B. This would cause the car to change direction as wheel A would slow down relative to wheel B. This is the same for light. One side of the beam of light will slow down relative to the other side as it enters a glass/Perspex block. This causes the beam to bend as one side is travelling at a different speed to the other for a moment.

> Note: If the car were to enter the mud head on (90º) and not at an angle, both wheels would enter the mud at the same time so the car would not turn. This can be seen when a light beam is shone straight through a glass block.

11) How does a ship calculate the depth of water it is sailing through?

Answer:
Ships use echo sounding to calculate water depth. They send a high-frequency pulse down from the ship to the sea floor. This pulse reflects back to the ship and by using the formula below the depth is calculated:

$speed \; \dfrac{distance}{time}$

distance = speed × time

Note: because the pulse has to travel to the sea floor and back we need to halve the answer, so the formula becomes:

distance = ½ speed × time

d = ½ vt

12) A ship uses echo sounding to calculate water depth. If the echo takes 0.95 seconds to leave and return to the ship and the speed of sound in water is 1300 m/s, calculate the depth of the water.

Answer:
d = ½ vt
 = ½ × 1300 × 0.95
= **617.5 m**

13) During and after an earthquake waves travel around the Earth. They travel as three different types of wave which can be destructive, but also support the idea of the structure of the Earth being in different layers and densities. Describe the different types of waves.

Answer:

Wave 1, the Primary (P) Wave

When an earthquake occurs inside the Earth, if it is powerful enough to crack or move layers of rock, then huge amounts of energy are released. This energy travels as a seismic wave. A Primary Wave is the first wave felt in an earthquake. It is longitudinal so it has the effect of moving the ground up and down at the Earth's surface.

Wave 2, the Secondary (S) Wave

An S-wave occurs after P-waves. It is a transverse wave. It moves slower than P-waves, and produces a side-to-side movement at the Earth's surface, shaking buildings, and is very destructive.

Wave 3, Long (L) Waves

Long (L) waves tend to be the most devastating at the Earth's surface. This is because they produce both up-and-down motion and side-to-side motion at the surface. They only happen in the Earth's surface in the mantle, they can't move through the liquid core.

14) i. Why do S- and P-waves change direction as they move through the Earth?

   ii. What is a shadow zone?

Answer:
i. After an earthquake, S and P-waves move through the mantle. Because the density of the mantle changes with depth, this causes the waves to bend. Primary waves will refract at the boundary between the mantle and outer core. Secondary waves don't refract because they can't travel through the outer core, as it is a liquid.

ii. A shadow zone is an area where the S and P-waves are not recorded by seismometers. Some seismometers will only record L-waves, however.

Colours of light and lenses

In this section we need to be familiar with specific scientific language as it can be confusing, so read question 1 carefully and learn the meanings!

1) Explain (define) the following words commonly used when we talk about light:
    i. visible spectrum
    ii. translucent
    iii. transparent
    iv. opaque

    Answer:
    i. Visible spectrum: A small section of the electromagnetic spectrum which can be detected by the human eye.
    ii. Translucent objects allow light to pass through them but light is scattered or refracted inside them. You can't see objects clearly through them; think about a 'frosted' bathroom window – it allows light in but gives you privacy.
    iii. Transparent objects allow light through them and none is absorbed or scattered. This is like a normal pane of glass.
    iv. Opaque objects absorb, reflect or scatter all light which shines upon them, so you can't see through them.

2) Why does a blue piece of paper look blue?

    Answer:
    Objects which are blue absorb all the colours of the visible spectrum except the blue section. A blue object will reflect the blue wavelengths of light. If a blue piece of paper were placed under a red light, however, it would look black because it would absorb the red light and reflect none.

    > Note: Black is the absence of light, i.e. no light reflected.

3) Draw diagrams showing the passage of light through convex and concave lenses.

Answer:

The convex lens

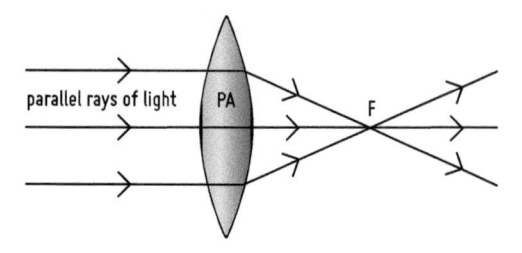

(the image is real which means it can be focussed on a screen).

P.A. = principle axis, which is a straight line which joins the centres of curvature.

F = focal point or principal focus where all the rays converge (meet)

An example of a convex lens is a magnifying glass.

Note: Always put arrows on ray diagrams and use a ruler.

The concave lens

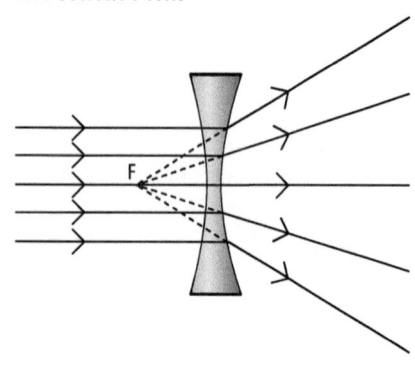

(the image is virtual)

Note the principal focus appears from an imaginary point and the light leaves the lens as if it were diverging from that point. Diverge means spread out.

4) Draw ray diagrams for a convex lens when:
   i. the object is between the lens and F (magnifying glass)
   ii. the object is between F and 2F
   iii. the object is at 2F
   iv. the object is past 2F

   Note: 2F means twice the distance for focal point F.

   Answer:
   i. Object between lens and F (fixed point)

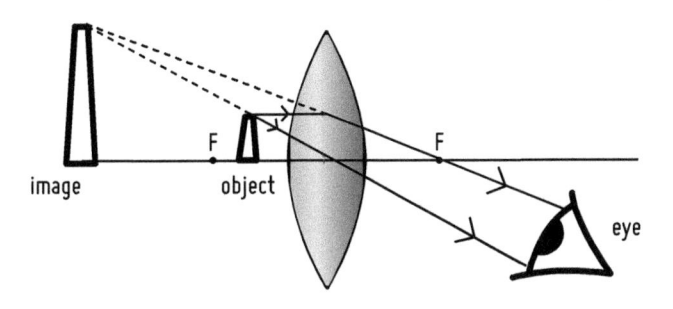

   The image is upright but virtual and magnified

   ii. object between F and 2F

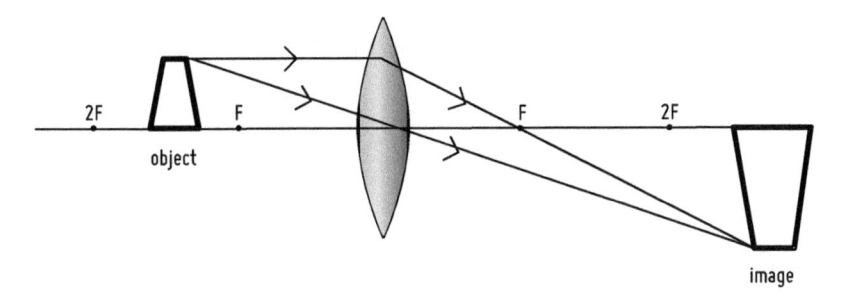

   The image is beyond 2F, it is upside down (inverted) and larger than the object

iii. object at 2F

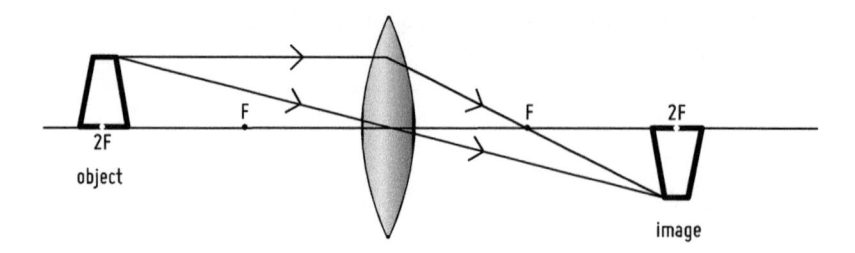

The image is inverted (upside down), same size as the object and is real so can be projected onto a screen

iv. object past 2F

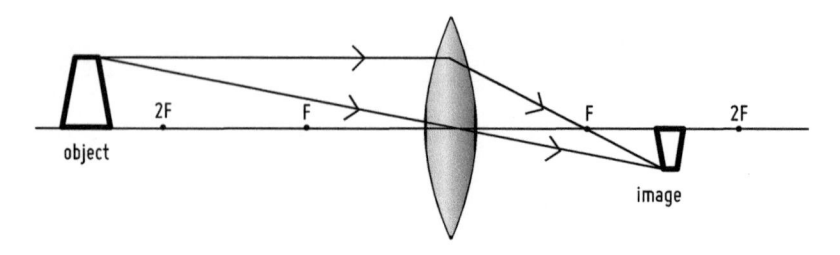

The image is smaller than the object, upside down and real.

Rules for drawing lens diagrams

1. Draw first line from top of object through middle of lens
2. Next draw parallel line to axis from top of object into lens. Then through 'F'
3. Where they cross draw the image

Short revision of waves and lenses

1) State the wave equation and all the units involved.
2) Name two types of wave.
3) What is amplitude?
4) What is a rarefaction?
5) What is a compression?
6) A wave has a wavelength of 10 m and frequency of 200 Hz: calculate its velocity.
7) What is an incident beam/ray of light?
8) What do we mean by the word 'normal' in ray diagrams?
9) Explain why light bends when it passes through a material of different optical density.
10) A wave has a time period of 2.4 seconds: what is its frequency?
11) A boat sends a high-frequency pulse down to the sea floor and receives an echo in 0.8 seconds. Calculate the depth of the water if the speed of sound in water is 1250 m/s.
12) Draw two diagrams showing how light bends as it passes through a convex and concave lens.
13) What do we mean by translucent?
14) Describe the image in a magnifying glass.

164 WORKSPACE FOR SELF-TESTING

Answers:

1) $v = f\lambda$ m/s, Hz, m

2) Longitudinal and transverse

3) The maximum displacement from rest

4) Where waves are stretched apart in a compression wave

5) Where waves are squashed in a compression wave

6) 2000 m/s

7) Ray entering a medium, mirror or hitting something

8) An imaginary line drawn at 90° to a mirror, glass block, etc.

9) See Q. 10 in waves section

10) 0.416 Hz

11) 500 m

12) See Q.3 in lenses section

13) Material which allows light to pass through but it is scattered so no image seen

14) Upright, virtual and magnified

SPACE AND THE UNIVERSE

1) What do we mean in Physics when we say 'the life cycle of a star?'

   Answer:
   Firstly, stars are obviously not living objects! They do, however, go through stages which we call a 'life cycle'. Stars fuse hydrogen nuclei together in a fusion reaction. When a star does this it releases huge amounts of energy as light and heat; when its fuel (hydrogen) runs out it stops, swells and collapses. Remember gravity plays a huge role in a star's size as every particle has a small gravitational pull, so combined together stars have a massive gravitational field. This can keep planets in orbit around them like our Sun does, keeping the Solar System in place.

2) Describe the two possible outcomes for the life cycle of a star.

   Answer:
   Stars are formed from enormous clouds of gas and dust called nebulae. Because each small particle of dust or molecule of gas has a tiny gravitational pull, they start to attract each other. A protostar is formed when enough matter and therefore gravitational forces are produced and the atoms of hydrogen are squashed together and start a nuclear fusion reaction. A star is born! The stars move onto a stage called the 'main sequence'. Our Sun is on the main sequence. The next step in the life cycle depends upon the amount of mass a star has.

   First option. Stars similar or smaller than our Sun:

   These stars will increase in size and change from yellow to red, becoming Red Giants. Heavier elements than helium are formed. Eventually as the helium has been used up, so the nuclear reactions stop. This means the Red Giant will cool down. Because nothing is being ejected from the fusion reactions, gravity becomes the dominating force so the Red Giant collapses in on itself forming a White Dwarf. Eventually the White Dwarf cools as all the fuel (hydrogen) has been used up and it turns into a Black Dwarf.

   Second option. This is for stars much greater in size and mass than our Sun:

   These stars enter the main sequence in the same way as all other stars. However, because that have a much greater mass they form Red Supergiants. They burn up their fuel (hydrogen) eventually and collapse, but because of the much greater gravitational forces and pressures they blow up in a gigantic explosion called a 'Supernova'. At the centre of a Supernova is a core which has such high forces neutrons are formed, so we call this a Neutron Star.

3) Draw a simple flow chart showing the two possible outcomes of the life cycle of a star.

   Answer:

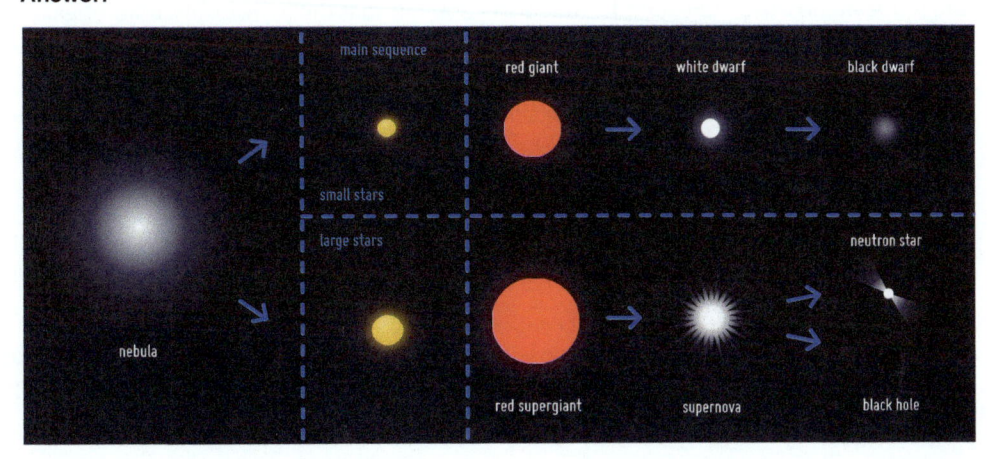

   [Flow chart showing: nebula → main sequence → for small stars: red giant → white dwarf → black dwarf; for large stars: main sequence → red supergiant → supernova → neutron star or black hole]

4) What is the Big Bang Theory?

   Answer:
   Simply put, the Big Bang Theory explains how the Universe may have begun. It started with a singularity which is a tiny point where a huge amount of mass is concentrated and the normal laws of Physics don't apply.

   Around 13 billion years ago this singularity exploded and all the matter in the Universe was thrown out in a very hot, dense cloud of atoms and energy. Space and time was created from this point onwards. Nothing existed before the Big Bang, not even time!

5) What evidence is there to support the Big Bang Theory?

   Answer:
   There are two pieces of evidence to support this theory:

   a) Red Shift
   b) Background cosmic radiation

Red shift

Astronomers study the stars and stellar objects by analysing light given out by these objects. This light is called 'spectra'. Visible light is made up of many colours or wavelengths, ranging from red to violet. When the light is studied it can tell scientists what the star is made from, for example. Scientists noticed that the light from different galaxies or objects had increased wavelengths the further away they were. When the spectra were analysed, thin black lines could be seen. This is where the light is reabsorbed at specific wavelengths. When the light spectra were compared to different sources, the black lines had moved. The wavelengths had stretched. Objects moving away tend to stretch the wavelengths towards the red end of the spectrum – hence the name Red Shift.

Objects, however, which are moving towards the observer, tend to bunch up in the other direction towards the blue end of the spectrum so are blue shifted. The wavelengths were being squashed.

Because objects are moving in every possible direction when observed, they show shifting wavelengths, this suggests the objects have come from a universal point, or explosion. This is evidence for the Universe expanding.

Lastly, scientists noticed that the further away an object is, the faster it is moving.

Background microwave radiation

Cosmic background radiation is in the microwave region of the electromagnetic spectrum. It is thought this radiation was originally gamma radiation which has stretched into the microwave region as it travels through the Universe. In 1965 scientists mapped this radiation and concluded it could only have come from a giant explosion from a single point in space (the Big Bang). If you detune a radio, the static you hear is this radiation interfering with your radio signal.

6) What are the possible fates of the Universe?

Answer:
There are currently three theories about the fate of the Universe. There is the 'Steady State' theory which suggests the Universe is static. The Universe has expanded from a point due to the Big Bang, then gravity pulling on all objects moving away balances the outward force so they become still. This is the Steady State.

The second theory is the 'Big Yawn'. This idea is that all objects are moving away from each other after the Big Bang. Gravity is not strong enough to stop them moving so the Universe will keep expanding forever.

The third theory is the 'Big Crunch'. This theory reads that all objects move away from each other to a point and then stop for a moment, as gravity and the force driving everything outwards balances. However, if gravity is the dominant force it will drag everything backwards, back to a single point and there would be an explosion again. This may happen on a cycle.

> Note: all the theories depend upon the density of the Universe. This is because each particle has a gravitational pull so they add up to a large overall gravitational pull. If we have a very dense Universe with lots of matter in it, we will have a Big Crunch. If the density is small compared to the explosive forces, then we will have the Big Yawn. If the density and therefore gravity are much the same as the explosive forces, then we will have the Steady State.

7) Why do stars remain stable on the main sequence then change to a Red Giant or a Supergiant?

Answer:
Stars on the main sequence have balanced forces or are in equilibrium. The force of gravity pulls the gases in towards the centre of the star. As energy and particles are ejected out of the fusion reactions they are flung outwards. As long as there is enough fuel (hydrogen) in the centre its own mass holds the star together. As the fuel is spent the gravitational forces decrease. Eventually gravity is not enough to hold the star together and the star will start to expand. Because the force of gravity decreases quickly with distance, this explosion once started will be quick. The route the star goes now depends upon its mass as previously described.

8) What is a satellite?

Answer:
A satellite is any object which moves around another object in a spherical path. There are two main types: natural satellites like the Moon orbiting the Earth, and artificial satellites like weather satellites used to predict weather conditions, or communication satellites. The force which holds satellites in orbit is called 'centripetal force'. This force is directed towards the centre of the object being orbited. A combination of a forward velocity of the satellite and centripetal force holds the satellite in orbit.

9) Why does a satellite's velocity change constantly but its speed stay the same?

Answer:
Velocity is a vector quantity which is derived from magnitude and direction. Speed is a scalar quantity, so is only dependent upon magnitude. As the satellite moves around the Earth its direction is constantly changing as it is always 90º to the direction of the force acting towards the centre of the Earth. This means its acceleration is always changing because acceleration is the rate of change of velocity.

10) What is a geostationary orbit?

Answer:
Satellites in a geostationary orbit appear to stay in one place above the Earth's surface. This is achieved by having the same orbital motion as the Earth's rotation. This is used for satellite TV, for example. A satellite dish on a building is fixed in one position pointing at the satellite. It does not have to move and follow the satellite across the sky. Communication satellites use this type of orbit.

11) What is a polar orbit?

Answer:
A satellite in a polar orbit moves around the Earth in a low orbit moving over the North and South poles. Because the satellite is moving in a vertical path and the Earth is spinning in a horizontal path, it means the satellite can cover the whole of the Earth's surface in one orbit if it has the right speed. Weather or spy satellites use this type of orbit.

Short revision questions on Space and the Universe

1) Draw a simple flow chart showing the life cycle of a star similar to our own Sun.
2) What is a nebula?
3) Describe what we mean by Red Shift in as few bullet points as possible.
4) What is the Big Bang Theory?
5) What is the Big Yawn?
6) What is the fuel for a star?
7) What is a geostationary orbit?
8) What is a satellite?

Answers:
All the answers can be found in this text!

WORKSPACE FOR SELF-TESTING

WORKSPACE FOR SELF-TESTING

174 WORKSPACE FOR SELF-TESTING

WORKSPACE FOR SELF-TESTING

176 WORKSPACE FOR SELF-TESTING